HOUSE
of VALUES & BEHAVIORS

ANDY ALBRIGHT & JEFF BRIGHT

Designed by Gwen Heginbotham

Edited by Jane Albright, Mac Heffner, Jay Daugherty

ISBN: 978-0-9973786-1-0

Printed in the United States of America

Visit my website at AndyAlbright.com. Thank You!

table of contents

disclaimer

This manual is meant for internal use only and is not for public circulation. In no way should any part of this book be reproduced in any shape, form, or manner. It should only be used within the company for the purposes of educating and training.

No statement, graph, illustration, or statistic in this book, shall be used as any type of contractual agreement, nor will it modify or serve as a supplement to any existing contractual agreements between the company, the author, or any member of the company. It is for example and explanation purposes only.

The contents of this book, which explains recruiting others to join our team, can affect individual commissions; therefore, the information contained within should not be used to gauge past or projected future earnings of individuals.

This book is only intended to serve as a guide to help individuals through the process of building a sales team. Only licensed insurance agents within the company should speak about products and services offered. All sales are made based on the needs, product sensibility, and financial affordability of the clients.

The strategies presented are based on 25 years of trial-and-error approaches. The information given is based on what typically has worked and what has not. Potential prospects are not required to purchase any products or services of any kind with the intention of becoming an agent.

Despite seeing numerous licensed agents experience highly successful careers using this system; this book is based on individual cases. A number of variables can impact results and income levels: work ethic, work patterns, dedication, persistence, activity levels, and many other factors. All participants achieve different levels, and these levels often change over time. An individual's true results cannot be predicted.

foreword

As the head football coach at North Carolina State University, I have the privilege to lead young men every single day. It's a role and job that I take very seriously, and I love coaching our players and staff.

When I think about what it means to be a leader, several things come to mind. A leader is someone who is going someplace, and they are not going alone. They take people with them on the mission and they have a goal in mind during the journey. Leaders help serve as a catalyst for others and help people achieve things they would not normally accomplish if they were on their own.

Leaders earn the trust of others, they set a clear standard of excellence, they equip people with the tools, resources and information they need to be successful. Most importantly, they set the tone by being the example of what is expected.

A true leader empowers others, and knows that you need great people with you if you are going to have a winning team.

During my tenure as NC State's football coach, I've been able to meet a lot of people who are successful. Some of them inherited that success, and some created it on their own. Andy Albright has built something pretty incredible with The Alliance. I feel fortunate to consider Andy a friend, and I have enjoyed getting to know him and watching him grow in the last five years.

In coaching, you find out quickly who has your back when things don't go your way. Whether we have won or lost football games at NC State, Andy Albright has always been there. I can't tell you how many times he has called or texted me at a time when I needed to hear an encouraging word. He is a positive influence, fiercely loyal, a true friend and a person that I greatly respect. Simply put, Andy Albright is a leader. A big part of being a leader is doing the right thing. It's about making sure people live up to the standards that have been established, and the whole team supports the mission.

I care a lot about Andy and what he has built at The Alliance. I encourage and challenge you to do your best because that's what Andy does every day. Don't cheat yourself, your family or your future. Ask yourself, "How good can I be?"

Our country needs your best, our children need your best and you need to be the best you can be. That's what leaders do. You are in position to be successful if you are willing to elevate yourself and commit to working toward your goals and dreams. Andy desires to help others be successful. He's created a system that allows people to succeed with The Alliance.

This book is another example of how Andy invests in people. "The Alliance House of Values and Behaviors" is a guideline for how you can succeed with The Alliance. Andy has now written a book that documents clearly how members of The Alliance are expected to act, behave and perform.

You can't build a great house without a great foundation. Your core values hold up your house. The Alliance has eight core values, and that is the major theme in the book you hold in your hands.

If I handed you a dictionary with 100,000 words in it, what word would define you? For me, it would be persistent. No matter what happens, I keep going. That's just who I am. I encourage you to be persistent in all that you do. Andy is also that kind of person. He keeps going, no matter what he is doing. He has set high expectations for himself, and he pushes people to perform at a higher level than they even thought possible for themselves.

I hope you take the information on the following pages and implement it in your daily life. I wish you success in all that you do, and hope this book helps you perform at a higher level than ever before. And as always- "Go Pack!"

DAVE DOEREN
NC State Head Football Coach

Introduction
OF THE HOUSE

Company culture is an integral part of every business and organization. It affects nearly every aspect of the company. From selling, recruiting, and building, it's the backbone of a positive climate. Within a positive corporate culture, many staff and agents find the real value in their work, and this leads to a variety of positive consequences for your bottom line.

A company's culture is its identity. It is how the company views itself, and how the company wishes to be viewed by the outside world. Building the culture you want is not quite as easy as you might think. Simply claiming some set of values and behaviors and plastering them on your wall won't build your culture. You must first define them so that there is no chance for misinterpretation, and then train your people to put them to use.

The Alliance, has created such a culture. In this book, we share our secret formula through the representation of a house. Our house is made up of three belief dormers: 1. Sell, Recruit, Build; 2. Have Fun, Make Money, and Make a Difference; 3. Duplication, Association, and Edification. Those beliefs are held up by our eight pillars (core values) of Excellence, Service, Integrity, Accountability, Respect, Compassion, Community, and Gratitude.

We have eight steps leading up to the door of The Alliance. Those steps of: Communicate, Be Accountable, Be Teachable, Attend All Meetings, Read, Listen, Work, and Personal Use give you all access, when followed to the door of our house. When the door is opened, this allows you to cross through the threshold into Prosperity, Inspiration, and Eternity (or what we call P.I.E.).

This book's focus is on the eight core values and the four behaviors or expectations behind each pillar (for a total of 32). These 32 behaviors exist as a guide to help a person understand the expectations within each of the eight core values.

Each of the core values were selected intentionally and specifically to provide and promote our belief dormers. Excellence and Community were put in place to help an agent Make Money. Excellence influences your ability to Sell, Recruit, and Build. Community addresses the need to Duplicate, Associate, and Edify.

Service and Gratitude were established to encourage an agent to Make a Difference. Integrity, Accountability, Respect, and Compassion exist to ensure we Have Fun. Our version of having fun is not about celebration, but rather learning to like each other. When we are comfortable with each other we have a tendency to gather easier as a collective we, team and family.

As an added bonus, the book contains an inventory (value perception profile) in the back. It is there as a way to measure which value you place preference on when managing your down-line. If you score below nine on any of the values, it is not an indication of a weakness in your leadership, but more of a reflection of your current strategy. Marks of above 11 on any of the eight is not an example on how well you effectively utilize that value, but rather, once again, an indication of your preference in the current environment or situation. Scores that stay between nine and 11 are indications of playing it safe with that particular value (not over utilizing or under utilizing).

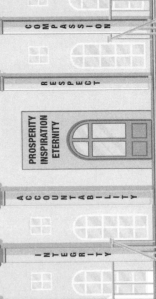

excellence

PRIDE
SHOWING UP ▶ DRIVE ▶ DISCIPLINE

WINNING SPIRIT
SOMETHING TO PROVE ▶ ENTHUSIASM ▶ AMBITION

CONTRIBUTION ▶ CONFIDENCE ▶ PERSPECTIVE

chapter

THE ALLIANCE PLAYBOOK DEFINITION OF

excellence

"SURPASSING ORDINARY EXPECTATIONS WITH DISTINCTION AND SUPERIOR QUALITY."

Excellence is when becoming **Indispensable** (distinction) meets extreme **Focus** (assurance of superior quality). Excellent-minded people get up everyday with massive curiosity and an overwhelming sense of confidence to tackle their day.

excellence

PRIDE
SHOWING UP

WINNING SPIRIT
SOMETHING TO PROVE

CONTRIBUTION
HONORING COMMITMENTS

Our first core value or pillar that holds up the House of The Alliance is Excellence. In order to demonstrate excellence within The Alliance House, one must accept the following formula: **Pride + Winning Spirit + Contribution.** We measure pride by showing up; winning spirit by waking up with something to prove; and contribution by honoring commitment.

albright's answers on excellence

Merriam-Webster definition of Excellence: the quality of being excellent. An excellent or valuable quality.

Excellence is a quality that is made up of a tremendous work ethic.

When it comes to people who were excellent in their professional and personal life, it would be hard to find a better example of excellence than the late John Wooden, who won 10 NCAA basketball championships in a 12-year stretch as the head coach at UCLA – including seven straight from 1967-1973 and four perfect 30-0 seasons. He was 620-147 in 27 seasons as the Bruins' head coach.

Coach Wooden passed away at age 99 in 2010, but left behind a legacy that carries on today through the lives of the thousands of people he touched in his life. His life is not only a model for basketball coaches, but for any person who wants to be successful period.

How did he become one of the greatest leaders of his generation? It started with habits, many of which he learned from his father growing up in Indiana. He learned the importance of habits at an early age, and he carried great habits with him as he became a great leader.

Do the best you can every day. Try to get a little bit better each day. You don't have to make astronomical improvements, but you should get a little better each day. If you keep making improvements, then excellence will eventually come your way.

John Wooden pursued excellence not national championships. Being outstanding means standing out. Being excellent comes with a price. Wooden never talked about winning. He was more concerned about being the best possible version of yourself.

"Success is peace of mind which is a direct result of self-satisfaction in knowing you made the effort to become the best of which you are capable." — John Wooden

Today is the only important day of your life. Yesterday is gone, it will never change. Tomorrow can only be affected by what you do in preparation today, and failure to prepare is preparing to fail.

If you are not excellent today, your goal should be moving toward the goal of becoming excellent. That happens by getting up each day and getting to work. Many people think consistency is boring. However, that very repetition is what helps move you toward excellence. If you can make what you do fun, then it will be easier for you to create winning habits that guide you to excellence. Master the mundane.

Make each day your masterpiece. That's how Coach Wooden believed you should live. He said it over and over to his players and coaches.

Make each day your masterpiece.

Take a minute and ask yourself, how can I make each day my masterpiece?

Do you live each day thinking about how you can get the most out of the 24 hours you were granted? Do you end each day thinking you did the very best you could with the time you had? Coach Wooden believed that success was about doing your best in all that you set out to do in a given day. That's what he believed was necessary to be considered excellent.

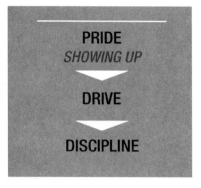

Let's now do a deep dive into the formula, starting with pride. What creates pride is a strong case of drive. Drive is the recognition of an opportunity and is motivated /capitalized on by a sense of urgency, a fire in your belly. But where does drive come from? It is fueled by our discipline. Discipline is our tenacity, a stamina to withstand anything thrown your way that is trying to distract you and keep you from moving forward. Tenacity is heated by consequence, which keeps our discipline from being drained.

Therefore, drive is protected by urgency. This is what we need for people to understand: there are consequences to their actions. For example, if you fail to "Do the Do" consistently then you are not going to win an incentive trip.

Pride is a virtue. A lot of people see pride as one of the seven deadly sins. It actually is the number one deadly sin; if you look at it from a negative connotation. Pride in itself is not a bad trait. Pride can actually move us closer to our goals.

Pride is a virtue, because it makes you more diligent; if you realize that you are good at something. This realization has to happen in order to kick start your pride. If you realize you can be good at this business, it creates an emotional state. This is what pride is: it is an emotional state created by the fact you realize that you can be good at something; maybe for the first time in your life. Consequently, guess what that does? It makes you say the magic words to yourself to get you moving: I deserve this.

So many people do not do this business to the fullest, because they do not think they deserve success in their life. Pride will assist you in revealing the feeling of not deserving. I wish and I pray that I had the power to give you partial amnesia to the stuff and the crap that has happened in your life, which has spurred on the dysfunction you presently struggle with. If I could remove those established memories from your brain, you could change your tomorrow immediately.

Pride requires a sense of self-worth, which in turn, causes one to take responsibility for one's actions. It also demands you to carry yourself with dignity which is displayed through the act of manners. Here is a quote by rapper Lil Wayne that best represents this: "And if you come up from under that water and there's fresh air, just breathe baby. God got a blessin' to spare. I know the process is so much stress but it's the process that feels the best. I came from the projects straight to success and you're next, just try, they can't steal your pride, it's inside. Then find it and keep grindin' cause in every dark cloud there's a silver linin.'"

Lil Wayne's process of allowing your pride to help you fight through the pain into the light on the other side can only be realized with an attitude of self-worth and behaviors laced with dignity. By taking responsibility for your life and not blaming, you can find the drive which lives inside of you. By displaying manners with a level of decorum, one will come to accept the secret sauce of success: a disciplined life. Being able to marry drive and discipline allows you to consent to a routine or habit in order to master the mundane.

PRIDE

"The light on you is not as important as the light that is in you."

- Author Unknown

Moral: Taking pride in your actions does not come from external praise, but rather radiates from the internal flame created by your own self-concept.

DISCIPLINE

"You will never always be motivated; so you must learn to be disciplined."

- Author Unknown

Moral: Your enthusiasm may have a short-term effect upon your drive; but your long-term fear of the consequences will sustain your mastering of the mundane.

albright's answers on pride

Inspiration is for amateurs. The rest of us just show up and get to work. The act of doing should become part of your daily routine. Now, you're playing offense and pride is your point guard.

Pride is the non-excuse one. Just get the ball in the basket. Get the bread in the oven. Get the puck in the net. Get the pigskin over the line. Show up on time. Pride separates excellence from mediocrity. By showing up with pride we gain stability with forward momentum. When you ride a bicycle you need speed. You can guide a geyser, but it is very difficult to motivate a mud hole. This momentum builds resistance to losing interest in the mundane.

A caveman can be good at this business. I know people that don't know everything, but make six-figure incomes. But I know people who know everything that cannot make dials. The reason why this is true is because their favorite word is, "I'm frustrated." I say shut up and start dialing!

WINNING SPIRIT
SOMETHING TO PROVE

ENTHUSIASM

AMBITION

The second part of the formula for Excellence is Winning Spirit. This is a special gift that you give to yourself. You need to get up every day with something to prove, not just to the world, but to yourself in order to catch this thing called the winning spirit (we call it "not being scared").

In 1910, President Teddy Roosevelt gave a speech that best typifies the winning spirit in The Alliance. Here is a part of his speech: "It is not the critic who counts; not the man who points out how the strong man stumbles, or where the doer of deeds could have done better. The credit belongs to the man who is actually in the arena, whose face is marred by dust and sweat and blood, who strives valiantly; who errs, who comes short again and again, because there is not effort without error and shortcoming; but who does actually strive to do the deeds; who knows great enthusiasms, the great devotions; who spends himself in a worthy cause; who at the best knows in the end the triumph of high achievement, and who at the worst, if he fails, at least fails while daring greater so that his place shall never be with those cold and timid souls who neither know victory nor defeat."

The winning spirit is kept alive by enthusiasm, which allows you to focus on your passion and do what you love with full vigor. If you do what you love, it sustains you. Having that passion for life and rejecting the notion of becoming comfortable with your success will push you closer to greatness. When you become comfortable, you will not achieve all the goals you were destined to accomplish. There is so much more in you than you are settling for. Therefore, enthusiasm produces an eagerness that permits you to look forward to the every-day tough decisions. This eagerness will kill any need to settle for less or look back with any regret.

Enthusiasm grants you permission to show the plan like it is the first time you are doing so, and like the last time you ever will. For example: in the Johnny Cash movie, "Walk The Line," when Johnny is trying to break into the music business, there is a scene when Sam Phillips (the famed record producer) says, "I want you to sing this song like it's the last time you are going to sing it, with some passion. You must be believable, that's what sells."

Each day is going to challenge you, but every day you must look forward to that challenge. This requires a passion or fire within, which motivates you to want to be put in the position to change an outcome during "winning time," as ex-NBA star Reggie Miller called it. This willingness to compete with yourself stirs a self-motivation through which you discover your motives (what incites you to take action to change your life for the better). But what creates this type of enthusiasm in a person? It is called ambition. Ambition is a desire for achievement; it's a state of mind. First, one must understand that there is a difference between achievement and success. Achievement is what we are looking for. It is hitting the marks we set for ourselves; the goals we strive to reach; and living up to our potential. Actually, we need both Enthusiasm and Ambition to manifest within your business.

Second, ambition is driven by the need for distinction. This is where most in the population fall short when trying to practice excellence. If you want to win at "winning time" and possess a winning spirit, you have to want to separate yourself from the crowd, not in a non-lovingly way, but rather wanting to see your scores at the top of the leaderboard. You see, this is what excellence does for you. It allows for you to accept this need for distinction; a need that never takes a holiday. It is a warrior-type spirit that follows you the rest of your life.

The winning-type spirit is best summed up in this quote by ex-Green Bay Packer football coach Vince Lombardi: "Winning is not a sometime thing; it is an all the time thing. You don't win once in a while; you don't do things right once in a while; you do them right all the time. Winning is a habit. Unfortunately, so is losing."

In conclusion, a winning spirit is part attitude and part execution. The attitude consists of the following mindset: The way you do anything is the way you do everything (treat each step of a long process as the most important, and realize each dial puts you that much closer to your goal, and that much farther away from your former self). Execution is measured by what you do at "winning time," what you do when the pressure is on. At this time, you basically have two choices: 1) Let life happen to you (wait on your miracle) or 2) Make life happen (be your own miracle).

WINNING SPIRIT

"Sometimes isn't always."

- Fred Rogers

Moral: People who have caught the attitude of the winning spirit all realize one thing: sometimes you fail, but not always. Treat each opportunity like it is the one that will change your life.

AMBITION

"Intelligence without ambition is like a bird without wings."

- Salvador Dali

Moral: Our enthusiasm is the gift of nature. Once these passions ignite, they turn into the main spring of human actions: Ambition. Without this ambition, your intelligence remains grounded.

albright's answers on winning spirit

Not waking up with something to prove is a choice you make each morning. The strength of your commitment to winning is determined by how much you honor yourself. If you have a winning spirit, you are going to get the results you desire.

At some point, I need to hear the words "I did" and stop hearing "I'm going to." I don't want to change the outcome and lose, I want to change the outcome and win. Catch the ball and then explain how the guy was interfering with you. Your job is to do your job. Don't worry about the referee doing his job until you first, 100 percent, complete your job. If you miss catching the ball, but they don't call the obvious interference, it can quickly turn into an excuse if you continually dwell on it.

Winning spirit is an attitude of "having to win" versus "wanting to win." In order to make that transition, you must "get your mind right."

CONTRIBUTION
HONOR COMMITMENTS

CONFIDENCE

PERSPECTIVE

The third part of the formula for Excellence is Contribution. This is measured by your commitment level. This reminds me of the story about the chicken and the pig walking down the street. They come upon a grocery store with a sign that reads: "Eggs and Bacon Needed." The chicken says to the pig, "I am all in. I will donate some of my eggs, if you donate the bacon." The pig says, "you are just making a contribution. I am the one who is making a commitment!"

Some people strive to separate contribution and commitment just like this in their own lives. But when your commitment level matches your amount of contribution, your results will go up. Pride and Winning spirit are very important, but Contribution is where the rubber meets the road. This is evident when: agents attend our events like HotSpots, Instant Thunders and National Conventions (showing up with pride); many of them stay around afterwards (catching the winning spirit); and some sustain their activity for months (honoring the commitment they have made).

Believing in something will encourage you to make a contribution, but until you marry it to a commitment, you will never be accused of standing for anything. Everyone believes in this, and everybody believes in that, but if I ask somebody to come to a meeting, they say, "I believe in your meeting, but I can't come to your meeting." Are you contributing or are you committed?

Are you more likely to honor a commitment to another person than a promise to yourself? A lot of you will show up for other people and do for others, but never do anything for yourself. What is the worst thing a friend can ask for you to help them with? Asking you to dedicate your entire Saturday to help them pack their stuff up and move to a new house. It is one of the things many of us never want to hear. One will sacrifice their valuable time, but ask that same person to attend a HotSpot or bring a guest in order to change their life, and they will not show the same level of effort as they did for another when volunteering sweat labor. The moral of this story is this: never tell a friend you have time and a truck, and always show up to HotSpots.

Discussing commitment and promise always reminds me of the Abraham Lincoln quote: "Character is like a tree and reputation like a shadow. The shadow is what we think of it; the tree is the real thing." The tree represents commitment (what we know to be real and true); and the shadow represents promise (what we hope for such as shade). We hope for the shade that it offers us on some days, but the tree and its foundation will always be there for you.

In summary, contribution (believing in something) must connect to commitment (standing for something) in order to demonstrate excellence on a daily basis. But this vital connection cannot occur without the confidence to act. This type of confidence is driven by two factors:

1) A permission to trust again. You must learn to separate your future from your past; and stop looking for old answers in new places. Then and only then, will you be able to connect to something bigger than yourself. One way to jump start the confidence in others is to simply tell them you are proud of them.

2) A belief that things can get better. This is referred to as hope. It sustains our actions by providing them breath. Most of us are looking for social confirmation that our presence has value, that we matter. Henry David Thoreau said it best: "All people want is not something to do, but rather something to be."

However, confidence (trust + hope) is not possible without a proper perspective on life. A healthy perspective is made up of two elements:

1) A sense of placement in this world must attach itself to our self-worth. This allows us to discover who we are and also recognize who we are looking at in the mirror reflection of life. Once again, Henry David Thoreau had it right when he said, "The question is not what you look at, but rather what you see."

2) A readiness to embark on new adventures. This is driven by initiative: that introductory step in order to set things in motion. It is a leap of faith

that we must have to jump into the deep end of the pool. Getting others to take initiative is simply accomplished by making the following plea: "We need your help!"

It is worth noting, as a disclaimer that confidence and perspective both have separate enemies. Confidence will be attacked by doubt and perspective by procrastination. Doubt left unattended will quickly turn into shame. That shame, left unaddressed, will cause one to disconnect from the pack. Procrastination unattended will quickly turn into an excuse. The excuse making, if left unaddressed, will cause one to start blaming others for everything.

CONTRIBUTION & COMMITMENT

"Unless commitment is made, there are only promises and hopes...but no plans."

- Peter Drucker

Moral: The level of your contribution is in direct proportion to the depth of your honoring a commitment.

PERSPECTIVE

"What you lose in the fire, you will find amongst the ashes."

- Old French Proverb

Moral: Sometimes a little destruction is what you need to get out of a rut. Spiritual people will say that God never closes a door without opening a window. If something bad happens in your life, don't dwell on the bad part. Look to see what you can find in the ashes.

albright's answers on contribution

We want you to put forth your best and do all that you can possibly do every single time. That's what we need people doing. We want you to learn to compete against yourself and not judge your performance based on what others are doing around you. This encourages us to take action in our lives. It cuts us open, we heal and we grow. It requires us to ask, "What else can I do, and how else can I win?" We are looking for a person who demonstrates excellence through their contribution by honoring commitments no matter what.

Here is a way to jumpstart this type of commitment: "just admit your flaws." Put them on a piece of paper, look at them and make a commitment to change those behaviors. Admitting your flaws provides awareness, which fuels your commitment level.

We want you to put forth your best and do all that you can possibly do. When you "contribute" you either experience results or you help someone experience success. That's what we need people doing. We need them making contributions to their financial future, and helping others to do the same.

THE 4 BEHAVIORS OF

excellence

BE DELIBERATE   *BE PROACTIVE*

SET THE BAR HIGH   *INVEST IN YOUR CAPACITY*

To be truly excellent at anything you must have an incredibly clear definition of what excellence is to you, what it will look like in your life and how you will measure it.

You must exhibit a level of discipline that most people are unwilling to put forth. Lots of people talk about excellence, many say they want to be more effective, successful, happier, and more joyful…but it is the rare person who applies consistent discipline in order to turn their plan into reality.

The amount of success you achieve in your life is directly proportional to the amount of action you apply to staying disciplined around your personal belief system. If you understand what level of excellence you want to achieve, but you don't apply much action and sacrifice; then the outcome is mediocrity. If you want to win the Olympic Gold in the 100 meters, then run really fast – faster than everyone else!!! If you want to win in life, excel really fast -- faster than everyone else!!!

"The price of anything is the amount of life you
exchange for it."

\- Henry David Thoreau

*Moral: The price of success or being the best comes with
the exchange of the sacrifice you are
willing to make.*

Be Deliberate

BE DELIBERATE	**BE PROACTIVE**
SET THE BAR HIGH	*INVEST IN YOUR CAPACITY*

Deliberate thinking is the first essential ingredient guiding the pursuit of excellence. To excel at anything you must have or develop an extremely high level of dedication, self-discipline, passion, joy or love for what you are doing. You must not only commit yourself pursuant to the goal of excelling, but you must also commit yourself to the act on a daily basis in ways that lead you to excel. It means setting clear personal goals and relentlessly pursuing them.

To excel at the highest level, your commitment level must move to the point at which the pursuit itself becomes the center of your life's purpose. Everything is opportunity/cost. If I go out to a movie before finishing my dials, what is the cost of that? Focusing with intention is the single most important mental skill associated with performance at a high level. Focusing with intention not only allows you to connect with your purpose, but it frees you to perform without being disturbed by distracting thoughts. You must free yourself from unnecessary internal or external interference to step into the zone for high-level performance.

To achieve your performance potential, you must become highly accomplished at focuing only on what is attached to your purpose. Successful execution of all tasks comes from your ability to train your mind and body to concentrate on what is within your immediate control. What people don't understand is that getting motivated and staying focused are two separate things. You must find purpose in your action or the duration of said action will suffer.

Set the Bar High

BE DELIBERATE   *BE PROACTIVE*

SET THE BAR HIGH   *INVEST IN YOUR CAPACITY*

Excellence is not about hitting the bar; it's about setting the bar. Excellence is not the same thing as "success" or "being the best." Being successful or the best is only true for one moment in time; it doesn't make your competitor any less excellent, or make you any less excellent when they surpass you for a day, month, or even a year. Being successful is good; but being excellent is better. You will know when you have surpassed the expectation and achieved excellence, when you find out what it is you are passionate about.

Excellence is "consistent" superiority of performance. It is not the product of a certain personality. Personality doesn't predict if you will be able to perform a task, it just predicts how you tackle it. Excellence does not come from some special inner quality.

"Talent" is simply a label we put on competency. We tend to mystify excellence, thinking it comes from "natural ability," thus creating an excuse for failure. In other words, excellence is developed through an increase of quality over other performers.

When we are motivated by the little tasks we perform each day (the mundane), we keep coming back and work harder each day, thus increasing the quality of our overall performance. Refining our technique or craft should be a daily practice. Much of success comes from simply showing up day in and day out.

Performers with a positive attitude tend to be harder working and more satisfied when they reach their goals. Excellence is guided by belief in your potential, your goal, the meaningfulness of your goal, and trust in your capacity to reach said goal. To excel you must believe that you are investing in something worthwhile and that you have a good chance of making it happen. Abraham Lincoln said: "I am not bound to succeed, but I am bound to live up to what light I have."

Be Proactive

BE DELIBERATE	BE PROACTIVE
SET THE BAR HIGH	INVEST IN YOUR CAPACITY

Excellence is not a set level of quality or perfection. It's an ever-changing dynamic and a moving target. Your dreams are fast and elusive, be prepared to run faster. The quality of your craft and serving today should not be the same as the quality of your serving yesterday. It should be increasing and moving forward, not stagnating.

Having a strong vision in place ensures your ability to maintain or regain a positive, effective focus on the ultimate long-term prize when faced with potential negative input and/or setbacks. These obstacles may be both external and internal, but the intensity of both are manufactured in your own head. Just remember that all true successes come from failure. It is is your ability to refocus and not dwell long in the memory of the failure, which will separate you from the crowd. This separation is what makes you want to be proactive.

Invest In Your Capacity

BE DELIBERATE   *BE PROACTIVE*

SET THE BAR HIGH   ***INVEST IN YOUR CAPACITY***

Excellence is also about growth and maturity. It looks like personal practice. If you feel as though you're "good enough," please re-check your approach. Excellence takes hard work and means we are continually getting better. Be aware of where you want to be and set realistic goals for yourself. Don't be content with staying where you are.

People rarely begin a sport or other high-performance pursuits with total belief in their capacity to execute tasks with precision. You often do not know what you are capable of doing. Success is strengthened by experiencing improvement, learning from others, receiving positive/constructive feedback, and feeling the support of others.

Success is further strengthened by developing essential mental skills associated with excellence. These mental skills enhance the quality of preparation and consistency of your performance. Mental readiness refers to a positive state you carry into learning and performing situations. Personal excellence requires that you become proficient at getting the most out of your daily learning and living experiences. This begins with a commitment to make the most of each learning and performance opportunity.

To excel at learning, performing, or living, you must project openness to learning and a commitment to personal growth. You must be humble and mature enough to engage in a continual life-long process of self-discovery and act upon those discoveries. Consistent high level performers are great at following their own best path. The trick is for this path to become natural so that you will be able to follow it consistently without much conscious awareness (where it becomes a habit). Aristotle wrote: "Excellence is not an act but rather a habit."

service

MATURITY		HEALTHY IDENTITY		MEANING & PURPOSE
RESPONSIBLE ATTITUDE	▶	MORAL AUTHORITY	▶	ALIGNMENT

OPTIMISM		TRUST		UNITY
POSITIVE OUTLOOK	▶	HOPE	▶	BOND

CIVIL COURAGE		MERCY		INTIMACY
SELFLESS BEHAVIOR	▶	GRACE	▶	AWARENESS

chapter

THE ALLIANCE PLAYBOOK DEFINITION OF

service

"PROVIDING SATISFACTION BY GOING THE EXTRA MILE."

Service is when **Courtesy** (satisfaction) meets **Devotion** (going the extra mile). Service-minded people get up every day looking forward to helping people and finding solutions.

service

MATURITY
RESPONSIBLE ATTITUDE

+

OPTIMISM
POSITIVE OUTLOOK

+

CIVIL COURAGE
SELFLESS BEHAVIOR

Our second core value or pillar that holds up the House of The Alliance is Service. In order to demonstrate service within The Alliance House, one must accept the following formula: **Maturity + Optimism + Courage.** The Alliance measures maturity by exhibiting a responsible attitude, optimism by presenting a positive outlook, and civil courage by displaying a selfless behavior.

albright's answers on service

One of the great success stories in the fast food industry in American history is Chick-fil-A and its founder S. Truett Cathy, who passed away at age 93 in September of 2014 in his home just south of Atlanta, Ga.

At a young age, Cathy was thinking of ways to provide service to others and, in doing so, he became wildly successful. As a boy, Cathy bought and re-sold Coca-Colas to people and turned a profit. According to Chick-fil-A's "The Chicken Wire" site, Cathy learned that a neighbor was buying Cokes elsewhere with the liklihood that refrigeration wasn't an option in her home.

Cathy knew he had to provide better service to attract more customers. The neighbor explained to him that he could sell more Cokes if he iced them down. He listened and, more importantly, took action!

He set up a Coke stand in his yard, chipped ice from his mother's icebox and the people soon followed to buy his ice-cold Cokes. One of his regular customers was the lady who lived across the street. This was one of the early examples of how Cathy knew serving others mattered.

Cathy, like many young men in the 1930s, delivered newspapers. He made it a point to treat each paper like it was the most important paper he had ever delivered. He was quoted as saying, "I delivered each paper as if I were delivering it to the front door of the governor's mansion."

Cathy made sure the newspapers were not tossed mindlessly in the bushes. If it rained, he made sure to find a dry spot on each customer's front porch every single time. When collection day came, Cathy was typically rewarded for providing such great service, even though he had little face-to-face interaction with his customers.

After opening the Dwarf Grill with his brother, Ben in 1946, customer service and building relationships were both at the core of what Cathy did each day. If a customer was in the hospital or had a death in the family, Cathy sent food to the family.

When Cathy began opening Chick-fil-A restaurants, he made sure his local franchise owners and employees treated each customer as if they were the president when they walked in a restaurant. In his book, "Eat Mor Chikin: Inspire More People," Cathy wrote, "You'd be eager to serve the president well, make sure he had a clean table, then go up and see if everything was all right, or if he needed anything. If you're willing to do that for the president, why not treat every customer that well?"

Service is about going the extra mile so that people will want to be around you. If you make people feel important, they will want to help you too.

If you have ever been in a Chick-fil-A, you know that if you say "thank you" to an employee, you will immediately hear them respond with "my pleasure." A lot of people find it corny to hear that familiar response, but where else do you hear people respond so kindly when you thank them for their service?

At the time of Cathy's death, the "Bloomberg Billionaire Index" estimated his net worth at $1.9 billion, while Chick-fil-A was valued at $5.5 billion. He grew the little chain he started in 1946 to more than 1,800 stores.

When you are working with people, are you thinking about how you can provide service to the best of your ability?

The less I can get you thinking about what you believe or think you know, the more I can get you focusing on the most simple tasks – which allows you room in your life for serving others.

If I can get you to do a little, then you can go through many holes, many houses, many hearts and provide much service. What is going to make us big is the attention to detail and small things. We are in the people business, and we must remember that.

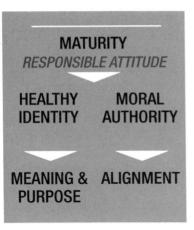

MATURITY
RESPONSIBLE ATTITUDE

HEALTHY   MORAL
IDENTITY   AUTHORITY

MEANING &   ALIGNMENT
PURPOSE

Let's now do a deep dive into the formula, starting with Maturity.

Maturity is the ability to respond in an appropriate manner (having discernment) according to the circumstances in one's surroundings. This approach must be tied to one's recognition of one's meaning and purpose in order to be successful. This recognition, therefore, correlates into a need to serve others.

This need is a move away from a cognitive approach when dealing with human beings to more of a moral development. This mean studying human behavior, but only focusing on human intentions from a place of moral authority (principles/truth).

Maturity has everything to do with the acceptance of not knowing as well as the replacement of the need to be right about everything. The older you get, the more you come to understand how your conscience works (a judgment which is less emotionally driven and more rationally based).

Your biggest weakness lives in your perception of people's perception of you. This false interpretation of reality exhausts your ability to focus on the service of others due to the unwarranted attention placed on the paranoia of "maybe."

"Maybe they don't like me," or "maybe they meant this or that." Maturity is when we stop worrying about the "unknowns" and start concentrating our efforts on the "knowns."

Maturity is also measured by the way you respond to something. It is learning not to make snap decisions, but rather choosing to act in an appropriate manner. The best way to behave in an appropriate manner is not abandoning who you are (rather demonstrating a "healthy identity"), and rising above the fray (by displaying a "moral authority"). In order to obtain and sustain "maturity" one must maintain a said, "healthy identity" (self-worth) and a said "moral authority" (wisdom).

A Healthy Identity or finding a fit/placement in this world is accomplished by discovering your "what" (meaning) and your "why" (purpose).

"What I am" is realized when you find something to do (action driven); and "Why I am" is realized when you find something to be (motive driven). Connecting the two (what and why) is vital when striving for a healthy identity or having a proper perspective (relative reflection).

This perspective of knowing that things "could always be worse" strengthens one's self worth and allows us to like ourselves. Liking what you see in the mirror is the last big hurdle after you rectify the "what" and "who" you are. This self-esteem that manifests from realizing your worth or value creates a crucial filter of judgment (maturity), in order to function in this dysfunctional world we live in.

"Maturity is not when we start speaking big things. It is when we start understanding small things." – Author Unknown

Moral Authority or observable and relentless "alignment" of one's values and actions is achieved by accepting your years of wisdom over minutes of emotionally clouded judgment. This type of "alignment" or "walking the walk" is executed by the following:

1) Honoring the opportunity
2) Obeying the rules
3) Acting with reason

Not walking the walk can result in the following negative traits: becoming judgmental, reactionary and resentful.

This recognition of one's influence (walking the walk) to impact future efforts of others is fueled by the following:

1) Personal commitment (Belief in the follow through)
2) Objectivity (Intention without bias)
3) Right conduct (Action laced in principle)

MATURITY

"Maturity is the ability to think, speak and act your feelings within the bounds of dignity."

- Samuel Ullman

Moral: The true test of your maturity is how calm you remain during the midst of your headaches. Maturity is the ability to respond to the environment in a good manner (with dignity). This response is generally learned rather than instinctive. Maturity also encompasses knowing when to act, according to the circumstances.

RESPONSIBLE

"The man who passes the sentence should swing the sword. "

- George R.R. Martin, author of "A Game of Thrones"

Moral: Take responsibility of your own decisions, never put them in the hands of others; be the first to own them. If you cannot bear to do that, then perhaps you do not deserve to make said decisions.

albright's answers on maturity

You have a moral obligation to serve the team. When we are in the house we have a responsibility to get a check and get the client covered. The agent has been given the authority to explain to them in a different way until they get it. In doing so, we must take the mature route of not screaming, but also not leaving without doing your do diligence.

You can get everything in life you want, if you help enough other people get what they want.

Maturity is best represented by your moral authority. Moral authority (or discernment) is understanding how to respond to your surroundings. It is learning to stay off your moral high-horse and keep rising above the struggle by taking the moral high ground. Your selfish agendas will erode your moral authority if you forget why you and I do what we do: Have Fun, Make Money and Make a Difference. Never let the following statement serve as your excuse: "I know what I was feeling, but I don't know what I was thinking."

When we are in the home we, as the agent have the responsibility to explain the importance of our products and to succeed at getting the client covered and leaving with a check.

The second part of the formula for Service is Optimism. It is a disposition or tendency to look on the more favorable side and to expect the most favorable outcome. This type of positive outlook creates a sense of hopefulness which in turn correlates into a service mindset. When you are in a happy state of mind, the more service-minded you become. But when you are unhappy and a dark cloud hangs over you, the more shut off and eventually unavailable you become to the world around you.

The best way to explain and understand the concept of optimism is through the words written Samuel Ullman (American poet, humanitarian and businessman, 1840-1924) in his poem, "Youth."

Here is an excerpt from Ullman:

"Youth is not a time of life, but is rather a state of mind. Nobody grows old merely by a number of years. We grow old by deserting our ideals. Years may wrinkle the skin, but to give up enthusiasm wrinkles the soul. Whether sixty or sixteen, there is in every human being's heart the lure of wonder, the unfailing child-like appetite of what's next, and joy of the game of living. When your spirit is covered with snows of cynicism and the ice of pessimism, then you grow old. But when you catch the waves of optimism, there is hope you may die young at eighty."

Trust and Hope are crucial ingredients in establishing one's confidence, as mentioned in the previous chapter on Excellence. But when both are combined in tandem they have a great impact on creating a positive outlook or Optimism. Trust comes from a belief in a bigger and better tomorrow, and Hope is a belief that life is a gift; as Mark Twain talked about using this gift as a service in his quote: "the best way to cheer yourself up is to try to cheer someone else up."

Trust originates from the likability state of Unity. Unity, when evident, exists in three forms: acceptance, agreement and alignment (the origin of moral authority).

When acceptance exists, it creates a safe environment (people start to not walk on egg shells). When agreement exists it promotes a supportive environment (people start to find common ground). And when alignment exists, it establishes strength in numbers (people start to have each other's back).

Hope originates from the uniting force of a Bond. A bond, when visible, manifests in the following three progressive stages: attraction, affection and attachment.

Attraction is distinctive by its first stage of connection, which brings forth an emotional state between members with a similar cause within a community or small group.

Affection is distinctive by its second stage of caring (or as Tim Goad calls it, "You matter!") which produces a courting state that allows members to feel their way through each other's likes and dislikes without bias or agenda.

Attachment is distinctive by its third stage of commitment, which lays down the foundation of a shared state, where members discover the power of mutual understanding in order to launch their new-found similar goals.

OPTIMISM

"Optimism is the ability to recap without apology and not complain when things don't go well."

- Author Unknown

Moral: Seeing the world or glass half full allows one to keep moving forward without defense of their position as well as not searching for excuses amongst their mistakes.

POSITIVE

"You cannot control what happens to you, but you can control your attitude toward what happens to you, and in that, you will be mastering change rather than allowing it to master you. "

- Brian Tracy

Moral: Stop worrying about what can go wrong and start considering what can go right.

albright's answers on optimism

Optimism leads to action and service. With appointments scheduled and 16 inches of snow on the ground, do you go or do you sit at home? With a negative outlook we cancel, but with a positive outlook we realize that everyone is going to be home, and it'll be fine. Hoping it will stop snowing and they will be home later is not going to change lives, and is not a demonstration of a child-like faith or appetite that turns optimism into service.

If you can catch the wave of optimism, there is hope that you may die young of spirit. If you can get an old soul of optimism when you are young, you will have a fresh soul when you are old.

It is crucial that we spread this spirit of optimism throughout our HotSpots. We need to create an inviting environment where newcomers are not worried about getting cut down or put down. There is strength in numbers only when, for example, 27 of us believe in the same thing (unity), and that 28th person comes in and experiences an emotional attraction to our team. They realize for the first time in their lives that they are not alone, and that everyone in the room has their back.

This is the beginning of what is called the sparking strategy, which is divided into two phases:

1) Honeymoon Phase
2) Unity Phase

During the honeymoon period you are introducing potential new agents to the greatness of our company. The message is simple: we care about you, and no matter what, you get another chance (there's always tomorrow).

During the unity phase we are still coaching, but the message is now: we are all in this together, but the expectation is you must pull your own weight. But, never losing the opportunity to point out that your success is my success.

It is this faith or trust that drives the spirit of dedication to others. When one dares to be hopeful, there is strength in one's vision of service founded in confidence.

The third part of the formula for service is Civil Courage. It is the demonstration of someone's free will (or choice) to stand up for something right or just. It is also a decision to take action, or willingness to recognize and confront issues/tasks in the face of popular opposition/discouragement as well as personal loss. With this display of moral courage comes possible negative social consequences which require one not to react to such attacks.

"Don't sweat it and don't stir it."

Civil courage is not simply a matter of trying to see through the lens of others (empathy) and imagining what they are going through (understanding), but having the testament to assemble enough courage to do something about it.

Theodore Roosevelt said it best: "Knowing what's right doesn't mean much unless you do what's right." Civil courage or displaying a selfless behavior is simply being faithful to that which exists already inside yourself. Isn't it strange that physical courage is so evident in our society but moral courage is so uncommon.

Civil courage is born out of two attributes: mercy and grace. Mercy is merited compassion toward the sinner. It is God not giving us the punishment we deserve (derived out of pity). Mercy allows us to express sorrow to someone's misfortune (a form of condolence).

Grace, on the other hand, is the unmerited favor from God toward the sinner. It is God giving us blessings we do not deserve (devoted toward the non-befitting). Grace allows us to award voice to someone's truth (a form of recognition).

The more we care for the well-being of others, the greater our own sense of true happiness becomes. In other words, this internal happiness or peace of mind fertilizes our selfless need to expose our buried, just beneath the human spirit, civil courage. Acceptance of the influence of mercy and grace makes civil courage an easy proposition. But for that to become a reality, one must first understand the origin of both mercy and grace.

There exists true mercy and false mercy. False mercy avoids the good pain (getting close to another) up front but ends with bad pain (loss of connection with another). It masks itself as safe, risk free, secure and pain free. But false mercy eventually enslaves us in our fears and keeps us from becoming a service to our fellow humankind.

True mercy, on the other hand, allows us to feel the compassion that lies within the condolence we speak. Instead of playing it safe, true mercy is the wedge buster to the barrier which "unlocks our safe" to the belief of service over self: intimacy.

This type of "customer intimacy" in business allows you to form a partnership and engagement with your clients on a deeper level. This value proposition offers the client a reason to provide you more referrals and return business. Relationship selling creates a client's willingness to share personal information and emotion as well as expectations for future transactions based on a long-term intimacy with you as their service provider.

Although traditionally thought of as a religious concept, the experience of grace is available and benefits all people who seek it. Grace is a state of awakening to the gifts of existence, life and service to man and womankind. This type of awareness is the beginning of liberation, abundance and kindness, because, when you know better, you do better. Grace makes pretty the ugly things in life. Grace makes you more tolerant of the misgivings and idiosyncrasies of others, which in turn, allows you to be better at providing customer service.

Your purpose in life is created by your priorities. If you are unaware of your priorities, you will be unaware of your purpose and your life will feel meaningless. When you awaken to grace, you automatically become aware of what you love. When your love then becomes your priority, it enhances your service efforts. Grace gives you a larger and greater perspective. It allows you to experience the delivery of unconditional love and service.

Grace is the state of awareness that sees that there is more than enough (abundance). Life gives us an abundance of blessings too numerous to count, which awakens our civil courage. This fuels our "oneness." This is the realization that your happiness is interdependent with the happiness of others (where sustainable service lives). From that intimacy and awareness, we can go out into this world seeing that each human is a manifestation from a divine spark. That divine spark can be seen in the eyes of each of God's human creations. It is evidence of a soul that resiides in everyone.

MERCY & GRACE

"A thousand times I've failed still your mercy remains, and should I stumble again, I'm caught in your grace."

- Music lyrics from Hillsong United

Moral: Mercy is the patience demonstrated by the compassionate soul, and grace is the endurance in the stormy days demonstrated by the forgiving soul.

CIVIL COURAGE

"Without courage we cannot practice any other virtue with consistency."

- Maya Angelou

Moral: Civil Courage is the first of all human qualities, because it is the quality which guarantees all the others. If civil is absent from the courage, then all the other virtues have no meaning.

albright's answers on civil courage

Civil courage is best captured in this military idiom: "where am I, where's my buddy and where's the enemy?"

Understanding this progression and the priorities set upon each, can assist you in making the proper choices when faced with adversity. Basically, the lesson here is how can you help others until you establish your own state of well-being? Get your act together and you will be able to coach and encourage others to avoid the obstacles placed there by the enemies or opposers to their success.

This type of opposition is always going to try to keep you down, but you need to stand for what you believe by demonstrating this pillar of character: civil courage. It allows you to fight without ever being baited into a reaction immediately after an attack. You have a civil duty to keep your cool and avoid clouded judgment. Your service to the team is dependent on you exhibiting selfless behavior. A person who is willing to undertake the discipline and difficulty of controlling their own ways, is worth more to our cause than a hundred that are insisting we cater to their selfish needs.

THE 4 BEHAVIORS OF

service

ACKNOWLEDGE ALL FORMS OF COMMUNICATION

GREET EVERYONE WITH ENTHUSIASM

ENSURE COMMITMENT THROUGH FOLLOW UP

SHOW MERCY TOWARD THE INJURED SOUL

Your attitude must be like my own, for I, the Messiah, did not come to be served, but to serve, and to give my life. (Matthew 20:28). Being of service to something – a person, a group, a community, a cause or a belief – means that you have chosen to engage without expectation of reciprocation. The selfless act is marked by a remarkable degree of maturity.

Maturity is never an end in itself. It is not enough to keep learning more and more. We must act on what we know and practice what we claim to believe. Learning without service leads to stagnation. Yet serving is the opposite of our natural inclination. But as we mature, the focus of our lives should increasingly shift to living a life of service. The mature person stops asking, "Who is going to meet my needs?" and starts asking, "Whose needs can I meet?"

No matter what job title you hold, how many zeroes you have in your paycheck or where you came from, the true meaning of life can be summed up in one word: service. The 14th Dalai Lama writes: "if you contribute to other people's happiness, you will find the true goal, the true meaning of life."

If all mankind would embrace this important universal principle (which is required for true progression of an organization), the greed, so prevalent in the world today, would disappear. This true progression includes transcending the ego and practicing unconditional love. This invokes an attitude of servanthood, which is remarkably sober and very undramatic. True leaders are not looking for the fanfare from their acts, but rather go along quietly searching for ways to serve others.

"If you can keep your head when all about you Are losing theirs and blaming it on you, If you can trust yourself when all men doubt you, But make allowance for their doubting too; If you can wait and not be tired by waiting, Or being lied about, don't deal in lies, Or being hated, don't give way to hating, And yet don't look too good, nor talk too wise:

If you can talk with crowds and keep your virtue, Or walk with Kings—nor lose the common touch, If neither foes nor loving friends can hurt you, If all men count with you, but none too much; If you can fill the unforgiving minute With sixty seconds' worth of distance run, Yours is the Earth and everything that's in it, And—which is more—you'll be a Man, my son!"

- Rudyard Kipling
From the poem "If"

Moral: If you can make "allowances" for the weakness of others and demonstrate a "forgiving" spirit, then the bond created by service will become a reality.

Acknowledge All Forms of Communication

ACKNOWLEDGE ALL FORMS OF COMMUNICATION

GREET EVERYONE WITH ENTHUSIASM

ENSURE COMMITMENT THROUGH FOLLOW UP

SHOW MERCY TOWARD THE INJURED SOUL

Just don't do it as good as you can, but also do it as quick as you can. Service must include addressing the different ways people communicate promptly. Your team wants their needs met and to be heard if they have questions, comments or complaints. That is the bottom line.

When this is provided with proper training, The Alliance will be able to grow a loyal base and we will find success. Team members seek reliable service that is consistent and can be counted upon. They also want things to be easy. The last thing they want is to have to jump through hoops or make numerous phone calls to you in order to get the answers they need, especially when in the home. Team members, who discover listening, will find that they are more able to build depth and width; and ultimately thrive more when they communicate quickly and effectively with their organization.

In addition, keeping your team informed of recent updates and announcements is imperative. It fosters a mutual trust and can boost morale. Establish communication with team members on a daily basis regarding their progress against the goals being set. Share information regularly. People need to know how to understand the information you share with them. So, it is your responsibility to provide concise clarity when building their capacity.

When practicing this internal communication within your group, you should not become an internal editor with little room for input or comments. Individuals expect their leaders to be visible and approachable and often would like to discuss how their business structure is doing and want to be taken seriously when they ask. Giving people a voice and ear is probably the most vital service you can provide.

Greet Everyone with Enthusiasm

ACKNOWLEDGE ALL FORMS OF COMMUNICATION

ENSURE COMMITMENT THROUGH FOLLOW UP

GREET EVERYONE WITH ENTHUSIASM

SHOW MERCY TOWARD THE INJURED SOUL

A positive attitude – optimism, expectancy and enthusiasm – makes everything in our business easier. A positive outlook will boost your team and supercharges them. An upbeat attitude does not emerge from what happens to you, but rather from the enthusiasm with which you interpret what happens to you. Being enthusiastic about what you can control and not sweating what you can't, is the best way to inspire and serve your organization.

Ignoring whiners and complainers while still showing them love may be your most difficult task. They would rather talk about what is irreparably wrong, rather than what to change to make things better. They can't bear to see somebody less happy and satisfied and will try to zap your positive energy.

The words that come out of your mouth aren't just a reflection of what's in your brain – they are programming your brain how to think. Therefore, if you want to have a positive attitude, your vocabulary must be consistently positive. Refrain from using negative phrases such as "I can't," "It's impossible," or "this will not work." These statements program you for negative vibes within your team. When anyone asks, "How are you?" rather than responding with "Hanging in there," or "Okay, I guess" respond with "Terrific!" or "never felt better!" And make sure you mean it! When you are feeling angry or upset, substitute neutral words for emotionally loaded ones. Rather than saying, "I'm enraged!" say "I'm a bit annoyed."

Keeping your existing team engaged and growing your team -- one at a time -- is the most important part of building a team.

Jonathan Lockwood Huie writes: "the success of a project is best predicted by the enthusiasm of its participant. So it is your job to make your enthusiasm contagious."

Ensure Commitment Through Follow Up

ACKNOWLEDGE ALL FORMS
OF COMMUNICATION

ENSURE COMMITMENT THROUGH
FOLLOW UP

GREET EVERYONE WITH ENTHUSIASM

SHOW MERCY TOWARD
THE INJURED SOUL

"When I say, I'll think about it, I really mean: I'll forget about it completely until you bring it up again." – Will Ferrell

The reason actor Will Ferrell's tweet was so funny was because it is so true. How often are we guilty of telling someone we will think about it only to never think about it again? Maybe you have been guilty of telling someone, "I'll be praying for you" and forget about it the next second. If you really want to impress someone, don't fall into the trap of forgetting about it. Instead, be intentional about following through with what you said you were going to do.

You are being measured. Your ideal prospect is measuring your actions against your words. This isn't so much a moral judgment, and your prospect isn't trying to play a game of "gotcha." Your prospect is keeping score because your ability to keep your commitments, folliwng up and following through on your word, is the simple best indication as to what they should expect from you regarding future commitments.

Also, failing to keep your commitments is an indication that you don't care about your team members time or their outcomes. It's easy to talk the talk when it comes to executing and keeping commitments; it's much more difficult to walk the walk. A big part of trust and service is caring enough that someone else gets the outcome they needed and expected. If your prospect doesn't recognize that you care by your actions, then your opportunity is lost. What is at stake without this level of service is your reputation.

Are you willing to risk something so valuable?

Show Mercy Toward the Injured Soul

ACKNOWLEDGE ALL FORMS OF COMMUNICATION

GREET EVERYONE WITH ENTHUSIASM

ENSURE COMMITMENT THROUGH FOLLOW UP

SHOW MERCY TOWARD THE INJURED SOUL

England's former Prime Minister Margaret Thatcher once observed, "No one would remember the Good Samaritan if he'd only had good intentions – he had many too."

Of course the Good Samaritan was a man in a story that helped an injured traveler that was beaten and left to die. Their liklihood of getting along and being friends was unlikely, yet the Samaritan did the right thing.

We may quote scripture and recite quotes on love and God, but unless we are willing to get involved in the lives of others we are just blowing smoke. The Samaritan treated and bandaged the wounds. He sat the injured man on his donkey. He took him to an inn and cared for him throughout the night. The Samaritan could have said to himself, "I give regularly to my church. I donate to the Salvation Army every Christmas. I have done my part."

But he didn't! As the scriptures say, he had compassion and he acted on it. The central message of this story is that, if we are to be good neighbors, we need to be more like the Samaritan. The implied message is to get strong financially and stay strong financially so we can have the means to act on our good intentions. Remember, the generosity of the Good Samaritan would have never been possible if he hadn't had money in the first place. Jesus concludes the parable with this admonition, "Go and do likewise." When we learn this lesson, you, The Alliance family, and the world surrounding us will be better for it – teaching others to choose "service over self."

integrity

DISCIPLINED CONSCIENCE
DISCERNING JUDGMENT

▶ GUILT ▶ GUIDANCE SYSTEM

▶ LOYALTY ▶ UNWAVERING COMMITMENT

AUTHENTIC MINDSET
CONSCIOUS SELF

▶ TRANSPARENCY ▶ OPENNESS

▶ SINCERITY ▶ REAL

ETHICAL COMPETENCE
CODE OF CONDUCT

▶ HONESTY ▶ TRUTHFULNESS AND WISDOM

▶ CONSISTENCY ▶ BELIEFS AND CONDUCT

chapter

THE ALLIANCE PLAYBOOK DEFINITION OF

integrity

"MANDATING EVERYTHING WE DO BE ETHICAL, HONEST AND TRANSPARENT"

Integrity is when **Character** (what God knows of us) meets **Reputation** (what others think of us). It is realized when telling myself the truth becomes just as important as telling the truth to other people.

integrity

DISCIPLINED CONSCIENCE
DISCERNING JUDGMENT

+

AUTHENTIC MINDSET
CONSCIOUS SELF

+

ETHICAL COMPETENCE
CODE OF CONDUCT

Our third core value or pillar that holds up the House of the Alliance is Integrity. In order to demonstrate integrity within The Alliance House, one must accept the following formula: **Disciplined Conscience + Authentic Mindset + Ethical Competence**. The Alliance measures disciplined conscience by having discerning judgement; authentic mindset by recognizing your conscious self; and ethical competence by abiding by a code of conduct.

albright's answers on integrity

"We ourselves feel that what we are doing is just a drop in the ocean. But the ocean would be less because of that missing drop."
—Mother Teresa

Merriam Webster definition of Integrity: firm adherence to a code of especially moral or artistic values.

Do you know who Anjeze Gonxhe Bojaxhiu was or what she did?
That's OK. Most people don't know her by her birth name. However, most people have heard of Mother Teresa (now Saint Teresa) of Calcutta, and they know she lived her life with great integrity.

She dedicated her life to helping people – specifically those who lived in poverty. It was her "personal mission to provide for the physical and spiritual needs of the poorest of the poor while living among them." Throughout her life, she put the needs of others in front her own wishes.
She gave far more than she ever received, yet is one of the most famous people in the world. My guess is that her heart was full because she believed and lived with great integrity and a servant's heart. There are countless stories told by people about small acts she committed in an effort to improve their lives.

Mother Teresa specialized in the branches of medicine, surgery concerned with childbirth, and caring for women who had given birth. She went to Calcutta where she opened an "air school for slum children and began to teach them Bengali alphabet and basic hygiene."

Her life, her time and all her money were used to improve the people and causes of those less fortunate. As word spread of the work she was doing, people took notice and realized she needed more financial backing to help even more people. This led to major financial support, which allowed her to further her mission to help those in need.

She often faced dangerous conditions and environments that could have led to her death, but she didn't stop what she was doing. She operated in a manner where she believed her life was worth risking to truly make a difference in the world.

In 1950, Mother Teresa founded the Missionaries of Charity, a Roman Catholic religious congregation with more than 4,500 sisters. They were active in 133 countries in 2012. They helped manage homes of people dying from HIV and AIDS, leprosy and other ailments. They fed people who otherwise would have had no food. They provided education for children and helped the poorest of the poor.

Upon her death on Sept. 5, 1997 at the age of 87, Mother Teresa had received an impressive list of honors. The list is quite staggering. She earned the Ramon Magsaysay Peace Prize (1962), Albert Schweitzer International Prize (1975) the Nobel Peace Prize (1979), Presidential Medal of Freedom (1985), numerous honorary degrees from universities and was canonized in September of 2016. More importantly, she impacted thousands of lives for the better and made an impact that will carry on for generations to come.

Mother Teresa once said, "If you are humble nothing will touch you, neither praise nor disgrace, because you know what you are."

She never had to worry about what she did in life because her integrity and beliefs were so strong. She didn't waver or stray from helping those in need, and she was rewarded by being allowed to help more people as her supporters learned more about her and the needs of her mission.

We believe strongly in integrity and the influence it allows us to have on people from all walks of life. When you encounter people on a daily basis, do you think first of how you can impact others or do you think about what people can do for you? The world could use more people thinking more like Mother Teresa did when it came to her integrity.

DISCIPLINED CONSCIENCE

DISCERNING JUDGMENT

GUILT   LOYALTY

GUIDANCE   UNWAVERING
SYSTEM   COMMITMENT

Integrity is the mother to all other virtues. It is a firm adherence to a code of moral values. It is incorruptibility and begins when we deal justly with ourselves. Integrity is the light that shines from a Disciplined Conscience (the first part of the Integrity formula). Such a light is evident in one's behavior by possessing a discerning judgement, which assists in distinguishing right from wrong.

There are two essentials that supply breath to a disciplined conscience: Guilt and Loyalty. Both have a role to play in moral philosophy as they are linked by a sense of duty to yourself (guilt) and others (loyalty).

Guilt (as a virtue) is the realization of your responsibility to yourself not to violate your internal moral code (or what some call your moral "ought to's"). This code over time develops into your moral compass. Such a compass allows one to display a "discerning judgement." One's moral compass is made up of: an acute awareness (self-examination of one's moral failings) and a restitute surrender (restoration of another's self-respect). This awareness provides a person the ability to feel remorse; and surrendering allows a person to practice forgiveness.

The aptitude to demonstrate remorse and forgiveness is at the very essence of your "moral compass." It is important to emphasize the role these two actions play in sparking the other virtues (core values) into existence. Guilt does not rely on remorse and forgiveness to produce shame but rather to deliver a fear of disgrace. This disgrace not only comes in the form of "failure" to yourself but in the form of failure to others. Fear of disgrace is characterized by a concern for honor, reputation, and guilt by a concern for a clear conscience.

. As we have established, guilt fosters the development of all other virtues. But what gives guilt the power to create such force in our lives? It comes from an internal Guidance System which resides within each one of us. It is just as important that one realizes such a system is our responsibility to evoke.

This internal mechanism serves two purposes: 1) forces you to be able to explain your actions and defend your position 2) allows you to discover the reason for the thought behind the desire. Our internal Guidance System is the communication junction point between our physical selves (including our emotional and mental bodies; and our soul or divine self (including our intuition and gut reactions). It is these emotions and intuitions which give our guilt a "wake up call" of sorts.

How does this internal guidance work? It responds to your dominant intent. Your intention for yourself as a whole, and your intention for how you wish to experience this world at any given moment, is held together by the guidance system. While assessing your surroundings, it helps you rectify what you are actually seeking. Your sensitivities, perceptions and warning signals are then wrapped in a protective covering of guilt which actualizes as a structural and logical map (or what was earlier referred to as your moral compass). The best way to shut off your disciplined conscience (or discerning judgement) is to simply resist your internal guidance system.

Just as cars have a GPS that helps us get where we want to go, so do our bodies and souls. Too often we ignore this life-directional system which we are born with. Very often when people state, "I feel in the zone today," they are experiencing an opening up of their guidance system. But when people say, "I feel a tightening, a constriction, a pressure in my chest," it is not a heart attack, but rather it is the anxiety they are experiencing when their guidance system is being closed.

Loyalty is the second necessary ingredient when trying to ensure a Disciplined Conscience. It is a strong feeling of support and allegiance; and what the Greeks referred to as the "heart" to all of the other virtues. Loyalty means commitment to a cause, a purpose or a person. It embodies the ability to stand behind one's convictions and promises. As Socrates said: "Be slow to fall into friendship; but when thou are in, continue firm (in your convictions) and constant (in your promises)."

It is these convictions and promises that are the essential elements in an Unwavering Commitment. This commitment is the origin to all loyalty. It requires priority thinking, which is the building block to exhibiting honor. Convictions come in the form of devotion, which is an obligation to a creed; and promises come in the form of faithfulness, which is an adherence to a pledge.

Devotion or being steadfast is demonstrated by a standing behind something or someone when you alone have nothing to gain. Woodrow Wilson said: "Loyalty means nothing unless it has at its heart the absolute principle of self-sacrifice." To serve is to give of yourself, to be a servant in the service of others, to make sacrifices so that others can benefit. These sacrifices asked of us are the true test of our devotion and loyalty. This type of person will be courageous and do the right thing, and will not betray a friend when a safer opportunity is available.

Faithfulness is not changing direction, but rather fulfilling your promises, being consistent and resolute. It means you are worthy of trust. Faithfulness not only builds trust but also binds us together with stability. Without faithfulness, there is no unity. We admire people who show devotion and dedicate themselves to a worthy cause, but we respect people that remain faithful when they have no good reason to do so.

GUILT

"When we judge our own heart guilty, if we treat it gently, in a spirit of pity rather than anger, encouraging it to amendment, its repentance will be much deeper and more lasting than if stirred up in vehemence and wraith."

- St. Francis de Sales

Moral: On gentleness toward ourselves, what we want is a quiet, steady, firm displeasure at our own faults. So then, when you have fallen, lift up your heart by humbling yourself without marveling that you fell.

LOYALTY

"Is it money? Is it fame? Is it comin down with the loud pipes and the rain? Big chillin, only for the power in your name. Tell me who you loyal to. It is unconditional when the 'Rari don't start? Is it love for the streets when the lights get dark? Tell me when your loyalty is comin' from the heart."

- Kendrick Lamar

Moral: Damned or Blessed; depends on who or what you are loyal to.

albright's answers on disciplined conscience

If you can't explain your actions, then don't do it. Instead, try to discover the reason for the thought that may lead to a fault. Try to figure out where it comes from and then try to reason out in your mind how you would defend such a position. If you can't find your own origin or defense, then how could you expect others to come to your side? Always be able to defend your move by thinking things through.

Sometimes you have to sit and think, "what are my priorities?" If you don't know your priorities, how do you know if you are not violating a principled path to your success. Without such priorities, one can never demonstrate an unwavering commitment. This commitment requires your devotion and child-like faith to the cause. This belief is best represented in your obligation to the creed or shield. But the belief is not just a belief in the company logo, but rather is measured by your standing behind the shield of The Alliance. You are not only obligated to do your best for yourself, but you are also obliged to be an integral part of the Alliance team and represent the shield every day. how you represent the shield every day. This faithfulness is supported by the promise you make to The Alliance team. Can you promise never to purposefully let each other down or to allow another to be left holding the bag?

Members must be able to see the commitment in order to commit to it. This type of "stickability" is necessary in order to make it a reality. This was never more true in the 1978 and 1979 seasons for the former NFL team, the Houston Oilers (now the Tennessee Titans). The Oilers under the leadership of Coach Bum Phillips went to the AFC Championship game two years in a row with the aide of his "hold on to the rope" motivational strategy. He simply cut up a rope in to 53, inch- long pieces and distributed them to each player. He then instructed each man to hold on to their piece of the rope. It was their accountability tie to each other.

The holding on to the rope signified: do your part and not let the guy next to you down. The unity that this one-inch rope created was magical and spread through the organization quickly. The fans caught on and adopted the rope as a prop to wave in a sign of support during the "Luv ya Blue" campaign. Props can be contagious if used to represent a cause. Just as our plastic ID bracelets can ensure an unwavering commitment when not taken off until a goal is achieved after a national event. Doing this serves as a visible respresentation to yourself and the team.

AUTHENTIC MINDSET
CONSCIOUS SELF

TRANSPARENCY   SINCERITY

OPENNESS   REAL

The second part of the Integrity formula is an Authentic Mindset. This state of being in touch with your conscious self occurs under the following conditions: 1) when you are true to your personality (acting like who you are through your behavior); 2) when you are true to your spirit (liking who you are through your attitude); and 3) when you are true to your character (knowing who you are through your awareness).

The act of conscious living is a fluid situation, forever dependent on the constant growth of your mindset. In order to achieve the authentic status, one must be willing to erase immaturity with wisdom; replace righteousness with understanding; and recover your why with a reason to become. Our growth is stagnant unless we choose to continue pursuing our own development. In order to live such a self-directed life, you first must decide you want to be in charge of yourself. But before such a decision, one must establish the kind of life one would like to be in charge of. It is my belief that whatever our life path, it should be governed by a conscious decision to be transparent and sincere. It is these two attributes (transparency and sincerity) when paired together, engineer an authentic mindset. Transparency is a state of honest communications and sincerity is a state of being. These two states create the state of presenting (authenticity).

Transparency is needed to produce trust and open dialogue. Its lack of hidden agendas and evidence of full disclosure defeats insecurity. This indicates that a person's motives are easily understood. It takes strength to be transparent as well. This strength takes its shape as the cornerstone of transparency called Openness.

The key to a transparent culture is openness. Three factors produce an open environment: 1) accessibility (easily available information and approachable leaders); 2) predictability (consistent repetition of a state and a uniform course of action; 3) legitimacy (acceptable to the law and based on sound reason). When these three factors exist within an organization the members of said society feel and gain a personal capacity to entertain new ideas as well as accept established customs.

One must first learn to be Real, or there is risk of losing your authentic self. It is important to remember before establishing your sincerity status; you have to be viewed as genuine. This is simple to do, but many people fail at it. When you are being real, you are behaving exactly how you would normally behave and you are not altering your behavior in any way. Being artificial, fraudulent or illusionary will eventually rip away at your credibility. Without that credibility no one will either trust or respect you moving forward.

TRANSPARENCY

"Sunlight is the best disinfectant."

- William O. Douglas

Moral: Corrupt behavior, if fed, will grow in concealment. It is the light of day that will kill it at its root.

SINCERITY

"When the pure sincerity forms within, it is outwardly realized in other people's hearts."

- Lao Tzu

Moral: A recognized genuine approach will always have the biggest impact on the heart of another.

albright's answers on authentic mindset

There is one thing that's real clear about The Alliance Inner Circle and the top 33 leaders. There's no "wondering" if everyone is on board with the methods on how to build massive profitability in their business. Methods like getting referrals before you leave a home are a given. But in order to be subject to such a method, one must buy into the integrity behind the oath to help people with their money. It is this openness with our clients which create the "speed of trust." The trust our leaders have with each other translates into the transparency we deliver, without agendas, to the families needing coverage.

This "Authentic Mindset" allows us to be faster with the clarity we hope to spread. The speed of an organization is directly correlated with the removal of concealment. It is evident in a culture where everyone knows the playbook and follows the plays being called. When there are missed calls (and there will be), a brief time out to clarify will remove any confusion. Removing confusion will enhance personal and team growth. Bring true to yourself and the team benefits all.

Remember what goes down the well comes back up in the bucket. When it goes into the heart correctly, it then comes out of the mouth right: "The mouth speaks what the heart is full of." But we need to remember before we speak that we should ingest the improper and scrub it with our hearts before returning fire. This is the only way we will be able to persuade the hideous and reluctant in the world.

Be real. Don't trick people. Be transparent. Be a helper. Be truly authentic.

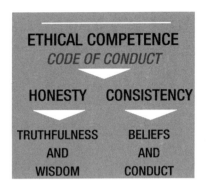

The third part of the formula for Integrity is Ethical Competence. It results from practicing a code of conduct that is ensured by Honesty (avoiding deceitful behavior) and promotes Consistency (creating prevailing standards of decency).

Ethical competence is the key distinguisher between simply having skills and having a true sense of professionalism. In leadership it simply translates as leaders displaying good character. An ethical leader with the right values can set an example for others and resist temptations that may occur.

Setting an example and resisting temptations may be the product of ethical competence, but the casual chain leading to its outcome is supported by honesty and consistency. Honesty sets in motion a force in your life that will push any dysfunction to the surface. Honesty is the evidence of our moral compass at work. It is heavily influenced by the positive and virtuous attributes of truthfulness and wisdom.

Truthfulness or straightforwardness is the quality that helps define the characteristic of being honest and telling the truth. Having a truthful nature about you allows one to connect reality to the truth. A truthful person, therefore, will be able to distinguish fantasy and reality. Once this difference is recognized as the truth, an honest person will always support said truth.

Another way to look at the relationship between truthfulness and honesty is: honesty is a product of the truthful nature of a person; and truthfulness directly fuels a person's honest nature. Both are used in order to explain each other. Thus, it is clear that both virtues cannot exist in independence. Honest people possess a reputation in society which comes from the moral fiber gained from truthfulness.

There are different shades of truth telling. When we tell "little white lies," we become progressively color-blind to the truth. It is better to remain silent than to mislead. It is that silence which originates from having great wisdom. You will not be able to realize your "wise" potential without producing "honest" thoughts.

I see ethics or a code of conduct as rules that come from an outside source. They are especially useful for people who have not yet grown in wisdom. Wisdom comes from the cultivation of qualities like compassion, love, patience, generosity, diligence, etc. As these qualities are developed, one will know how to act in the moment (applying the principle virtue of honesty, for example). At that moment, ethical competence becomes less important, and becomes more of an effect of those said qualities within your individual code of conduct or moral compass.

The second half of the recipe for Ethical Competence is the attribute of Consistency. Being consistent requires one to be norm compliant. This act encourages you to accept being uniform (creating regularity). Regularity soon leads to habit and habit leads to routine. Inviting routine into your life is the secret source to success called: Mastering the Mundane. Uniformity when practiced with regularity causes accuracy in our beliefs and our conduct.

Your beliefs are supported by your word. Your conduct is supported by your reputation. Your word is best represented by what you say. Your reputation is best represented by what you do. If your reputation precedes you, it means people have heard things about your beliefs or words. If your words are pure of thought and without malice, then you will not carry a bad reputation and be notorious for the wrong reasons.

HONESTY

"If you search for tenderness
It isn't hard to find
You can have the love you need to live
But if you look for truthfulness
You might just as well be blind
It always seems to be so hard to give
Honesty is such a lonely word
Everyone is so untrue
Honesty is hardly ever heard
And mostly what I need from you"

- Billy Joel

Moral: People are quick to offer compassion but find it difficult to follow it up with honesty. True wisdom starts with the recognition of the importance of honesty.

CONSISTENCY

"If a man vows a vow unto the Lord, or swears an oath to bind his soul with a bond; he shall not break his word, he shall do according to all that proceedeth out of his mouth."

- Num 30:2

Moral: Once a person connects their beliefs (word) with their conduct (reputation), they are bound by a pattern of predictable behaviors.

albright's answers on ethical competence

You have got to be honest to be wise. You have got to be wise to be honest. In order for this to be a reality, it must be done within a code of conduct and done with dogged consistency. Others do not judge you on what you say you are going to do, but rather on what you actually do. Taking a shower is not just a one-time thing, it is consistently done day in and day out.

It takes a tight inner circle of uniformity to build an army. This means you must practice every day being your brother's keeper. It means you are responsible for your HotSpot; the attendance, the enthusiasm, the message, the environment And if your brother (who is in our Army) is not covering his fox hole, then its your duty to politely tell him: The biggest lie being told is that you have time. Wasting time has an irreversible effect on the legacy you want to leave. Doing what you can, while you can, ensures the legitimacy of your efforts. It is this legitimacy which cements your legacy. A legit and honest effort will give you creditibility with your organization every time. It will be hard to ignore and invites others to model this behavior.

"Saying what you mean" is about being consistent with what you are thinking and the words that come out of your mouth. On the other hand, "meaning what you say" is representative of the words you select and how they correlate with your actions. I hear what you say, but I watch what you do. My ears hear, but my eyes watch.

In other words, "saying what you mean" borders heavily on assertiveness. Don't beat around the bush. In addition "meaning what you say" borders heavily on keeping your word. It is the commitment of being straightforward.

One may believe because someone's reputation is great that their character is also great. In this case, someone's integrity is to be determined. In The Alliance, we will believe you until you show us different.

Your integrity initially is tough to detect but its absence typically appears rather quickly. Bottom line—in all areas of life—it's better to have integrity than not. Kinda like its better to have teeth than not.

THE 4 BEHAVIORS OF

integrity

KEEP YOUR WORD *MAKE FAIR DECISIONS*

GUARD YOUR REPUTATION *ESTABLISH AUTHENTICITY*

What exactly is Integrity? According to the dictionary, integrity is "the quality of possessing and steadfastly adhering to high moral principles or professional standards, and the state of being complete, sound or undamaged." In order to remain a whole person you must set your course to an established, ethical set of principles that require your full attention and unwavering commitment. This attention must be honest and truthful and reflect the accuracy of one's actions. This commitment must be reinforced with a morally passionate belief in uprightness.

How do we know we are lacking integrity and operating with selfish intentions? We know by paying attention to our feelings. Our feelings are our inner guidance system, letting us know when we are thinking and behaving in ways that are in alignment with our essence, and when we are not. We know we are acting with integrity when we feel full, peaceful and joyful. We know we are acting in bad faith when we feel empty inside from the guilt we are experiencing.

The reason that so many people can behave in ways that are not in line with their integrity is because they have chosen to ignore their conscience, or have become numb to the feeling of guilt. When we choose to avoid our inner guidance system, then we start operating from our wounded self, behaving in ways that may harm ourselves and others. Your wounded self thinks that you can get away with trying to control and manipulate your moral compass, but not recognizing your inner guidance system is like numbing your hand with Novocain and then cutting it with a knife. You might not feel the pain at that moment, but later you experience the worse feeling of regret. Operating with integrity prevents this feeling of sadness, repentance, or disappointment over something that has happened or been done.

"One of the truest tests of integrity is its
blunt refusal to be compromised."

- Chinua Achebe

*Moral: Integrity is about not yielding to temptations
when they come. Doing the right thing when no one is
looking may not be enough. You might have to do the
right thing when everyone is looking in order to be a
person of integrity.*

Keep your word

KEEP YOUR WORD   *MAKE FAIR DECISIONS*

GUARD YOUR REPUTATION   *ESTABLISH AUTHENTICITY*

Words are powerful forces of creation. They take our dreams and goals and put them out there for all the world to witness. Florence Scovel Shinn, a metaphysician of the 1920's said, "There is always plenty on man's pathway; but it can only be brought into manifestation through desire, faith or the spoken word." Every time we speak, we create a road of some sort. The quality of that road, and how far it goes, will be directly related to the integrity of our word.

One of the first places integrity issues show up is in our language patterns. When we are "in integrity," we speak from a place of wholeness. Our words match our actions. As Dr. Seuss put it, "We should say what we mean and mean what we say." When we break from this pattern and say things we don't really mean, we are more "out of integrity."

Language is combines with work ethic meant to power our dreams into physical reality. When we spend our language on half-baked ideas, or passionate views we may have heard about but have no direct experience with; and we use language destructively or we say things we don't really mean, we lose personal power. Personal power comes from being in integrity and diminishes whenever our integrity is undetermined. Unfortunately, very few of us are taught the skills of using language as an integrity–building force.

To find the roots of our dishonesty with ourselves, we need only look as far as our cultural patterns around language and lies. Most of us consider ourselves good people. Yet most nice people also lie quite frequently. What lying does, as a rule, is to create multiple realities. The more lies you tell, of course, the more multiple realities you create and must live with. That's an enormous responsibility. It can also be energy draining, because it literally costs you integrity – the state of being connected, sound, consistent and undivided.

When enough "white lies" are floating around in your midst, your integrity becomes fractured. You may feel pulled in a thousand directions, and unable to make decisions without the fear that all these "custom made" realities could come crashing down around you. You may also not feel like you fully know or trust yourself at times. This can lead to some confusion about what is "real" and what is not. As we grow older, we discover this works. It becomes easier and easier for us to tell these white lies as a way of avoiding the discomfort of seeing or knowing what we feel we should not, the shame of being different or the fear of being ridiculed. Unfortunately, this dependence on lying in order to create comfort can deeply affect our ability to be true to our word, and our sense of personal integrity.

But how can we stop? "Speak with Integrity." Avoid using the word to speak against yourself or to gossip about others. Use the power of our word in the direction of truth, honor of your promise, and from a place of love.

As Biblically stated, Death and life are in the power of the tongue. -Proverbs 18:21. Choose your words wisely and keep your word to yourself and others.

Guard Your Reputation

KEEP YOUR WORD

MAKE FAIR DECISIONS

GUARD YOUR REPUTATION

ESTABLISH AUTHENTICITY

If I could teach only one value to live by, it would be Integrity. This means doing the right thing at all times and in all circumstances, whether or not anyone is watching. Building a reputation of integrity takes years, but it takes only a second to lose, so never allow yourself to ever do anything that would damage your integrity. Contrast that with the person who cannot be trusted as a person of integrity. Warren Buffett said that he looks for three qualities in an employee: integrity, intelligence, and energy. And if you don't have the first one, he said, the other two will kill you.

A word of advice to those who are striving for a reputation of integrity: avoid those who are not trustworthy. Do no associate with them. Do not make excuses for them. Do not allow yourself to get excited into believing that while they may be dishonest with others, they would never be dishonest with you. It also is important to realize that others pay attention to those you have chosen to associate with, and they will eventually judge your character by the character of your friends.

Inevitably we become more and more like the people we surround ourselves with day to day. If we surround ourselves with people who are dishonest and will cut corners to get ahead, then we will surely find ourselves following a pattern of first enduring their behavior, then accepting their behavior, and finally adopting their behavior. If you want to build a reputation as a person of integrity then surround yourself with people of integrity.

Make Fair Decisions

KEEP YOUR WORD   *MAKE FAIR DECISIONS*

GUARD YOUR REPUTATION   *ESTABLISH AUTHENTICITY*

Fairness is a hard concept for people to understand. It includes being able to see from another's point of view. Because most humans are egocentric, they see the world from their own perspective. They are not able to see another's position. This is a difficult proposition for another reason: fairness does not mean equal. It is a fact that life is not always just for all, but The Alliance seeks equality for all that seeks success through our proven system.

We demonstrate our fairness when we are not biased and show no favoritism. We demand fair treatment in all situations as we believe that we are equals and deserve impartiality when trying to make our dreams come true. Hard work is the greatest equalizer in our culture.

Establish authenticity

KEEP YOUR WORD

MAKE FAIR DECISIONS

GUARD YOUR REPUTATION

ESTABLISH AUTHENTICITY

Authentic means from the source or origin. Being authentic in a spiritual sense means as expressed directly from the source, through the soul. It is the raw, naked, unhindered expression of beingness of the soul. Authenticity is a quality of being. That is why we say "being authentic" not "doing authentic."

E.E. Cummings wrote: "It takes courage to grow up and become who you really are." Authentic people do not allow their fears to prevent them from being themselves. If you are focused on being true to yourself in every moment, you are less concerned about the potential for rejection from others. Nothing is more liberating than being yourself as fully as you know how.

Being authentic is a daily practice. It is a moment by moment choice of embracing your truth and being fearless enough to share it with the world when you have nothing to hide. When you can freely be yourself with everyone, there is a profound peace and confidence you will exude to the world.

 **accountability**

LIABILITY
OWNERSHIP ▶ BLAMEWORTHY ▶ ANSWERABILITY

OBLIGATION
DUTY ▶ DEFERENCE ▶ PROMISE

ESPONSIBLITY
AUTONOMY ▶ SELF-DETERMINATION ▶ CHOICE

chapter

THE ALLIANCE PLAYBOOK DEFINITION OF

accountability

*"STANDING BY OUR PERFORMANCE AND ACCEPTING
RESPONSIBILITY FOR OUR ACTIONS AND REACTIONS"*

In other words: Accountability is when **Commitment** (standing by obligations) meets **Willingness** (accepting liability). Accountability should expect to be assessed on progress (duty) and deliverables (ownership). It is the keenness and moral imperative to answer for one's resolution (commitment) and measures (willingness).

accountability

LIABILITY
OWNERSHIP

OBLIGATION
DUTY

RESPONSIBILITY
AUTONOMY

Our fourth core value or pillar that holds up The House of the Alliance is Accountability. In order to demonstrate accountability within The Alliance House, one must accept the following formula: **Liability + Obligation + Responsibility.** The Alliance measures liability by taking ownership; obligation by honoring duty; and responsibility by being autonomous.

albright's answers on accountability

"Leadership isn't about simply being in charge and treating your people like soldiers and barking orders. Leadership is sharing your knowledge and your direction so that others grow and reach their potential."- Cal Ripken Jr.

When you think about accountability, what comes to mind? You probably think of a person in your life who is or isn't the ideal definition of that word. We all have people, responsibilities and obligations whether we like it or not. When you are part of any team, you have tasks that must get done in order to be successful. To be your best, you have to set goals and you need people around you who will hold you accountable and push to do your best every single day. Part of being on a team is being a teammate. Ideally, you want to assemble the best teammates you can find. That's how championships are won.

The best teammates lead by example. They are accountable. They push people to succeed. They love to win. They expect others to give 100 percent and they do the same in return. They show up to work consistently. They seemingly do it over and over, time and time again.

Does the number 2,632 mean anything to you? If it doesn't that's OK. Unless you are big baseball fan it really shouldn't.

That's the number of consecutive games that Cal Ripken Jr. played for the Baltimore Orioles during a 16 ½ year run. How's that for being accountable to your job? Ripken decimated the previous record of 2,130 games by New York Yankee Lou Gehrig, a streak that most baseball people thought would never fall.

At old Yankee Stadium, Gehrig's monument read "amazing record of 2,130 consecutive games should stand for all time." Gehrig's mark stood for 56 years.

How was Ripken able to play so many games in a row, when for 56 years nobody else did? He loved his job. He was accountable to himself and his teammates. He wanted to do everything he could to help the Orioles win.

Ripken's streak started on May 30, 1982 when the Orioles still played in

Memorial Stadium, long before the streak ended at fan-friendly Camden Yards on Sept. 20, 1998.

It lasted five presidential terms. Ripken played for three different Orioles owners and eight managers – including Cal Ripken Sr. Through bumps and bruises, good teams and bad … Ripken kept coming to work. He played through it all. Every single game.

The streak ended when Ripken decided to sit out the Orioles' final home game of 1998. He broke Gehrig's record on Sept. 6, 1995, yet he continued to take the field for each and every game. Why? A column by Ken Rosenthal published in the Baltimore Sun the morning after the streak ended said the following: "Mark down the number -- 2,632. No one will ever play that many consecutive games again. No one will even try. What people will remember is the physical stamina, mental strength and incredible fortune it took for one man to play so many consecutive games. Iron Man, Family Man, Man of the People -- Ripken was all of those things that night, just as he has been virtually his entire career.

The Streak was his destiny. The Streak is his legacy."

Known for his dogged preparation, some people think Ripken was afraid not to play every day. Maybe he didn't like the unknown of what might happen if he took a game off? One thing is clear: Ripken certainly knew how to hit, run, throw and catch.
He earned the nickname "Iron Man" during the streak where he shined in the field, earning 19 all-star selections and two Gold Gloves and was twice named American League Most Valuable Player at shortstop and third base for the Orioles.

When the lineup card was handed to umpires before each game, Ripken's name was always penciled in because he was one of the best and his teammates and managers knew with him playing, the Orioles had a better chance to win than if he didn't play.

Ripken was accountable to his teammates and himself. He gave everything he could to help the Orioles win during his career. When he retired, he was rewarded by being inducted into the Baseball Hall Of Fame in Cooperstown, N.Y.

What if all of us approached our daily responsibilities and tasks with the same vigor and accountability as Ripken Jr. did for so many years?

I believe holding yourself accountable in all that you do will lead you to performing at a higher level, and it will also raise the productivity of your teammates. I encourage you to work on finding ways to be more accountable. People will take notice, and they will be more likely to follow your lead.

To be accountable one must: take ownership of their mistakes (liability); be duty-bound to their results (obligation); and accept the autonomy that comes with their decisions (responsibility).

This is a huge psychological thing that keeps people on track: owning, being duty-bound and accepting. Most of the time people keep on track because somebody is making them stay the course. But in order to get people to sustain their action and effort, it must be because they are ready to become "blameworthy," practice "deference" and have "self-determination."

When accountability and commitment come together, it will create a high level of focus. Your daily activities will then be in alignment with your targeted goals. In order to create a high ROI (Return On Investment), one must decide how much time today do to allocate to drive massive results for later down the road. We need people with the sense of being able to look into their own future and who can handle the autonomy that comes with becoming an entrepreneur.

Let us now do a deep dive into the formula, starting with Liability.

First, Accountability is the answering to or accounting for your actions and results. It is something you choose to exhibit -- it is not assigned to you. Accountability is the nerve center that runs throughout every successful human being. This nerve center is where the real power of accountability comes from (allowing individuals to focus on achieving results without being distracted and pre-paring excuses). Your daily activities must be in alignment with the targeted results. It is this type of accountability that ties commitment to expected results. Commitment forms a bridge between your accountability and your ability to be accountable.

Liability is basically letting your "actions" rise above your excuses. It is a buck-stops-here mentality. These "actions" of personal ownership are made up of:

- Buy in - Belief in the action (Trust in the system)
- Investment - Skin in the action (Vested belief in the system)
- Engagement - Pursuit within the action ("Doing The Do" using the system)

Maintaining all three of these actions allows you to take ownership or control of your actions so that your actions won't own you.

This simply means being bound (liability) to a debt (obligation). Too many leaders get caught up in thinking about power rather than their debt or respon-sibility to those they lead. You have to be willing to invite open criticism and own it in order to practice liability. Even at the risk or subject to experiencing something usually unpleasant, you are willing to take ownership and welcome becoming blameworthy. One must be willing to be blameworthy before allow-ing themselves to be liable, however.

Blameworthy is being culpable for one's actions. Once this takes place, you have given yourself the power now to make a necessary change. It allows you (in this progression) to:

- See Your Action
- Own Your Action
- Solve Your Action
- "Do The Do"

Blaming others only reveals one's own insecurities. Becoming responsible for your actions, allows us to reclaim our innocence and self-worth. As Aristotle notes; "if the wind picks you up and blows you somewhere you don't want to go, you're going there is involuntary, and you shouldn't be praised or blamed for it. Generally, we don't hold people morally responsible for events outside their control." This generalization has exceptions, though. You're still blameworthy if your irresponsibility puts yourself in a position where you lack control, such as through spontaneous reactions and unwelcome thoughts. In this case, deserving blame or criticism is from what is called "culpable negligence."

Richard Dawkins writes on this subject: "Ignorance is usually a passive state, seldom deliberately sought or intrinsically blameworthy." Robert P. Lawry continues this dialogue: "If you choose not to know something, especially if that something is something you should know, you are morally blameworthy." It is this type of blameworthy which requires a person to practice answerability (the trait at the root of accepting blame).

Answerability is being able to explain or justify one's actions. It is the ability to think before you act by saying to yourself: Just because I can do something, should I? This acknowledgement of reality makes you answerable for what you choose to believe to be true. It is that truth which drives a person to be accountable.

Making others practice accountability without applying the threat of answerability will not result in ownership of the action; a process necessary to solve a problem, or a challenge to the status quo.

Like the foul-tempered Queen of Hearts in Alice in Wonderland, who, at the slightest offense or misdeed cries "off with their heads," we all need a queen forcing us to report. That queen can take a form of a taskmaster from an outside force or manifest internally in the form of moral responsibility. Either way, we all need that reminder she provides.

LIABILITY

"We can easily forgive a child who is afraid of the dark; the real tragedy of life is when men are afraid of the light."

- Plato

*Moral: Being able to **respond** to the call of duty and **answer** for your decisions afterward, are the two key criteria when embracing the light of accountability.*

DISCIPLINE

"You either walk inside your story and own it or you stand outside your story and hustle for your worth."

- Author Unknown

Moral: You either take ownership for your actions or you spend the rest of your life covering up your mistakes with blame.

albright's answers on liability

Blaming others reveals one's own inner insecurities. By being in control of your actions, this allows one to reclaim their innocence and self-worth. It requires you to think before you act. This is going to be the biggest problem you will have when you earn a high income. If you cannot handle a problem on a little level, then you will never get to handle it on a bigger level. Being responsible allows you to practice "answerability" which is simply being able to justify your actions (standing up for your decision and being proud of that decision at the same time).

Navigating the waters of answerability first relieves us of having to go back and figure out why we chose this path. You will not have time to sit around and think of excuses, because you will not take time to take a breath. You will then start to say things like, "I ain't got time for that anymore; no piddling."

OBLIGATION
DUTY

DEFERENCE

PROMISE

The second part of the formula for Accountability is Obligation. Your obligation or sense of duty is measured by your external performance, which is actually just a reflection of your internal commitment. This commitment (duty) requires you to display willpower (the establishment of a marker).

The challenge, on your journey to practice obligation, is to remain curious while staying persistent, by taking more territory each day with an exuberant spirit.

As duty refers to moral commitment, it denotes an active feeling for doing something. Once a person engages themselves with some duty, or have been entrusted with a duty, then that person fully commits themselves to it. In the case of duty, the person will be involved in activity without any self-interest. As a citizen of The Alliance Community, a member must adhere to the ways of our established culture.

It is this sense of duty that makes it a seamless transition. Duty is a word that has been derived from the Old French Deu meaning which is "owning." Taking ownership in your community is evidence of your duty at work. But it takes great deference to apply this duty. Deference is the submission or yielding to the judgment of the establishing whole (The Alliance Community).

Obligation can only be realized if we learn to pay deference or homage to the greater will. Once one can learn to display great deference, one will gain their point by silence rather than trying to use words to talk their way out of something. Deference is the most elegant of all compliments. It requires great maturity as it demands all of us to suspend judgment, making it not important for us to always be right.

It is true, when the ancient playwright Terence said: "Deference gets you friends, honesty gets you hated." Keeping your mouth shut and doing your duty, without the need to weigh-in on everything, is the best litmus test for deference. Respect and politeness allows one to get on with the business of being obligated to an action instead of adding drama to action. But an expression of deference will not sustain itself without the promise to a cause.

This declaration of intention to honor a cause or commitment is the fertile ground needed to feed your deference demeanor, which in turn, permits your sense of obligation to grow strong. "Tomorrow brings anticipation with the guarantee of a promise but brings dread when delivered as a threat." (Quote by Jeff Bright)

The "anticipation" for the capacity of good to occur can only drown the energy-draining "dread" of what could occur, by honoring the internal contact of promise to oneself. Then and only then, can an exchange of promises even be possible.

Keeping a promise is an extension of honesty. In relationships, as well as business, keeping a promise bounds the individuals. It keeps the relationship intact, whereby failing to do so, can crush and destroy the relationship. Yet, no promise is fulfilled unless deference is paid to one another. If promise is the seed and deference be the gardener, then obligation or duty to the cause is the flower. And being obligated to your goals and objectives in life is an excellent way to show "accountability." A broken promise has led to the many demise of people not remaining accountable and finding someone to blame. It is a slippery slope from a promise not being kept to becoming exempt or immune to the dignity found in remaining accountable.

OBLIGATION

"To realize one's destiny is a person's only obligation."

- Paulo Coelho

Moral: To exercise one's obligation to said destiny, a person must first be able to recognize destiny's opportunity when it shows its face.

DUTY

"The sense of obligation to continue is present in all of us. A duty to strive is the duty of us all. I felt that call to that duty."

- Abraham Lincoln

Moral: Hearing the call is accepting the road to obedience. Realizing the rewards of serving are greater than any hardship. The call is a tug on the heart, persistently whispering for you to honor your commitments. People can try to ignore the heart tug, and even block the ever-present call with activity full of distractions, but if we listen, we cannot escape this call to obey.

albright's answers on obligation

Your external performance is a reflection of your internal commitment. You actually reveal your internal commitment (duty to yourself and to your team) by the numbers you reflect on the leaderboards. I say: "give it to me so it fits in a box." In other words, give me the number because the number tells me the drama. I do not need to hear the drama, just show me your results. The numbers also reflect your willpower during the process. It tells me how fast you can overcome hardships during trying times.

Practicing willpower gives yourself permission to be accountable. Willpower is the face (your face) of discipline. I can see your self-discipline in your willpower. The challenge is to remain inquisitive while remaining diligent. Every time I get on a big plane, I don't believe this thing is going to get off the ground. It blows my freaking mind. There is no way; it is inconceivable to me that we are going to leave earth and get back down on earth in one piece. But nevertheless, I never slow down my commitment to enter the plane.

It is this child-like curiosity or amazement that each day everyone awakes to a world where you have another chance; "another shot." This mentality is a tough one for everyone to maneuver, because once we think we deserve this shot, we start to believe that we are right about everything. Your child-like nature starts to be affected by your ego, and then you lose your aptitude for "deference." Paying deference or humble submission/respect is the evidence of your maturation process. It is the sign of true growth in a human being. Deference is like practicing good judgment.

Practicing deference (honoring of the collective we) can appear in contrast to the entrepreneurial spirit. That spirit produces a need to keep moving forward, getting others to grow, insisting that they have a duty to grow and not just stay where they are at and bleed. But the contrast exists when you are not also concerned with your team members growth and productivity. When jealously or contempt creeps in for our fellow Alliance brothers or sisters, then our ability to pay deference or recognition to their contribution becomes difficult. Applauding or marveling over each other's effort feeds the praise that people are thirsty for. Cash contests are not just about padding your bank account, but also about building self-confidence, which in turn, causes people to want to take more accountability for their actions.

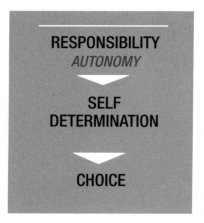

The third part of the formula for Accountability is Responsibility. Accountability and responsibility are often used interchangeably, but these words have distinct meanings that separate them. It is imperative that leaders understand the difference between accountability and responsibility if they want to move their organizations forward. Responsibility is task-oriented and something you are in charge of at the moment. Accountability is what happens after a situation has occurred and the expectation is or is not realized.

Responsibility focuses on defined roles and processes put in place to achieve a goal. On the contrary, accountability is being committed to the successful completion of tasks. When a result is not achieved, that is when most of us start hearing words like "responsibility" and "accountability." While responsibility is appreciated and often used to praise effort, accountability continues to be misperceived and gets attached to success or failure; and the explanation of each. We appreciate the difference in the definitions of both responsibility and accountability, but there is something truly empowering and not something consequential, when both are used synonymously and applied equally. The misapplication and separation of the two concepts can unintentionally create tendencies to blame, add unnecessary confusion, cause disengagement, and lead to poor performance. In other words, every organization needs people to own their action (accountability) and take action (responsibility) at the same time.

However, responsibility can produce ambiguity (vagueness and uncertainty) and become the Achilles' heel of accountability, unless specificity is managed. Defining clear expectations enables you to raise the standards of others. People need to "feel" in control of their goals. This "feeling" is a product of the autonomous mind (when you are free to make a choice within the playing field, promoting the entrepreneur spirit). This "need" manifests itself into one's self-determination.

Self-Determination assumes that all people have an innate tendency toward controlling their own growth (the what); self-integration (the why); and psychological consistency (the feeling). Your "growth" is measured by competence gained and thirst to maintain that growth and improve. Your "self-integration" is motivated by your ability to relate to an action and your recognition of a want. Your "consistency" is realized when your actions become congruent with your wants (the product of an alignment of your conscience and desire).

Self-Determination is your fundamental right to freely decide your own status and freely pursue your own development. It is your own declaration of independence of the rights of man and womankind. It is this ability to make decisions for yourself, which allows you to take "responsibility." The authority to have control over your life, the support to guide you through tough decisions, turns on your personal switch to take responsibility for determining your future.

All people need to develop these skills that arise from self-determination, but many also need help to learn how to direct their energy productively. This help comes in the form of internal motivation, when one learns how to exercise their own free will or "choice." This does not mean to be independent but rather autonomous -- which means exercising your right to make decisions that support your interests as well as your values. Ultimately, taking responsibility is rooted in your ability to choose your own fate. But most are afraid of this path since our own determination (from start to finish of a task) is reliant upon our sense of self and the freedom that comes with it. "Most people do not really want freedom, because freedom involves responsibility, and most people are frightened of responsibility." -- Sigmund Freud.

However, the notion that humans possess the concept of free will and self-determination has been ongoing since the beginning of recorded history. Free will (choice) and self-determination contain a lot of non-secular attributes to the notion that God gave man free will to choose their desired path in life. Both provide the insight that an individual's actions are conducted at their own discretion, and that the individual becomes self-determined for choosing to do the act. Lastly, it is important to remember that free will must be the precursor to self-determination. Without free will, the self-determined individual will not see themselves as blameworthy despite the fact that they did something they know was wrong. Free will supported by divine intervention is actually the real moral compass, which guides our actions.

RESPONSIBILITY

"The price of greatness is responsibility."

- Winston Churchill

Moral: If you want to be great, if you want to be a leader; then you are going to have to be the one to take responsibility for empowering others making decisions.

AUTONOMY

"I find it very, very easy to be true, I find myself alone when each day is through."

- Johnny Cash "I Walk The Line"

Moral: Autonomy and responsibility are clearly interrelated. Autonomy is a prerequisite of responsibility. Autonomy occurs when a person announces their willingness to take ownership for the consequences of their own actions. Because in the end, when they are alone with their principles, it is they that are making the "choices" that they must live with.

albright's answers on responsibility

"People will rise and fall to meet your expectations." Simple and clear expectations. Expect the best from people and inspire them, and they will rise to meet your expectations. We need to develop a more positive attitude, a more abundant heart toward people in order to get them to take on more responsibility.

For example, awarding agents Good Samaritan Bonus checks (The Alliance's bonus program to support charities) helps jumpstart the heart by teaching them the beauty of taking responsibility for the cause of others. When this occurs one begins to see the "relatedness" between themselves and the rest of the universe. This is somewhat the justification of why I go so strong. My "why" is driven by my belief in P.I.E. (prosperity, inspiration, eternity). I believe there is going to be a day when I am going to be accountable for what I did while I was on earth. I feel that this huge "why" overpowers my piddling excuses. My "why" keeps me from slipping and backsliding.

I want you guys to share this opportunity with people that have a good job and are looking for a great opportunity. But most of all, I want you to find potential agents (team players) with a big "why." When you find a person who has nothing and they are looking for a job instead of an opportunity, then you are going to fight that mindset with them. People searching for that opportunity to exercise their "free will" may not go as fast as you would like at first, but are less likely to argue with you along the way. But people with only active employment as a goal tend to be an active critic along the path of working our system. Anyone can succeed at the system if they apply the training provided.

Critics tend to ignore their responsibilities. They are better at being back seat drivers. They love to tell you how to drive but never want to take the wheel. They also enjoy advising me about why my logic is not right and why my P.I.E. is out of line, but never make the commitment to pursue this opportunity full time. These individuals really need to embrace their autonomous spirit, where they learn to be appropriately silent and comfortably alone in their own thoughts, and not trying to force others into a self-imposed prison.

THE 4 BEHAVIORS OF

accountability

BE SELF-DISCIPLINED   *TAKE OWNERSHIP OF YOUR CHOICES*

THINK BEFORE YOU ACT   *BE A SELF-STARTER*

Accountability is the guiding principle that defines how we make commitments to one another; how we measure and report our progress; how we interact when things go wrong; how much ownership we take to get things done. It is, in essence, the nerve center that runs throughout every part of the organization, through every working relationship to every member of every team.

The real power of accountability comes when the focus is on taking greater personal accountability for achieving results. That personal accountability manifests itself as greater personal ownership, buy in, investment, and engagement. When you take personal accountability, you own it. You tell yourself, "this is mine, I have got the ball." You ask yourself, "What else can I do to make progress, overcome obstacles and achieve the results?" You don't waste time blaming others or waiting for someone else to solve your problems. You actively engage and deeply pursue solutions yourself.

Consider this new definition of accountability: a personal choice to rise above one's circumstances and demonstrate the ownership necessary for achieving desired results – To see it, own it, solve it, work it and do it. The first step toward creating this kind of culture of accountability is to define clear and concise results. Everyone must know what they are working for and how their personal effort pushes the company forward. Each person's daily activities must be in alignment with the targeted results and goals.

"He that is good for making excuses is seldom good
for anything else"

– Benjamin Franklin

*Moral: Excuses provide the reasons to stop
your forward motion. Once you stop, progress
can not be realized.*

Be Self-Disciplined

BE SELF-DISCIPLINED	*TAKE OWNERSHIP OF YOUR CHOICES*
THINK BEFORE YOU ACT	*BE A SELF-STARTER*

Vince Lombardi said: "The difference between a successful person and others is not a lack of strength, not a lack of knowledge, but rather a lack of will." Willpower is your ability to set a course of action and then have the guts to engage. Willpower, therefore, is the spearhead of self-discipline. It is a concentration of force. It is when you gather up all your energy and make a massive thrust forward. But don't try to tackle your problems and challenges in such a way that a high level of willpower is required every day. If you attempt to use it for too long, you will burn out.

So if willpower can only be used in short powerful bursts, then what is the best way to apply it? How do you keep from slipping back into old patterns once the temporary willpower burst is over? The best way to use willpower is to establish a beachhead, such that further progress can be made with far less effort than is required of the initial thrust. Remember D-Day – once the Allies had established a beachhead, the road ahead was much easier for them. So you need to learn from the lessons of this significant event in history. Take a little more territory each day so that it is much easier to continue moving forward from this new permanent change in your progressed position. Using your willpower in this fashion is like establishing that beachhead on the shores of your goal.

Remember, don't use your willpower to attack your biggest problems directly. Rather, use your willpower to attack the obstacles whatever they might be (bad habits, lack of knowledge, lack of training, etc.) that perpetuate your problems. Fortify your position with a new habit. Habit puts action on autopilot, such that very little willpower is required for ongoing progress; allowing you to practically coast toward your goal.

Think Before You Act

BE SELF-DISCIPLINED   *TAKE OWNERSHIP OF YOUR CHOICES*

THINK BEFORE YOU ACT   *BE A SELF-STARTER*

The most important key to making wise decisions is consequences. Every single decision you have ever made or will ever make has consequences. Once we learn to evaluate our decisions based on consequences, all the other considerations fall neatly into place. It's that simple. Even your internal sense of right and wrong will be satisfied if you apply this simple process: Follow your decisions to their logical conclusions before you make them.

The life you are leading today is the result of past decisions and indecisions. If you don't like your current situation, change the way you make decisions. Many people make decisions based on instant gratification with no regard for long-term consequences. This is what I call the kamikaze approach to life. It is the opposite of wisdom.

Others blame their situation, rather than accepting responsibility. In this case, their actions are being hindered by their excuses.

Then there are those who postpone making decisions because they are waiting for the right circumstances (a perfect storm to happen). In reality, that is just one aspect of an avoidance technique we call procrastination.

We must realize, however, that before we act or don't act, we may never know for certain what the consequences will be. Therefore, we should take care in considering what will result in the most ethical decision.

Take Ownership Of Your Choices

BE SELF-DISCIPLINED

TAKE OWNERSHIP OF YOUR CHOICES

THINK BEFORE YOU ACT

BE A SELF-STARTER

Only when you accept full accountability for your thoughts, feelings, actions, and results can you direct your own destiny; otherwise, someone or something else will. The real value and benefit of accountability stems from the ability to influence events and outcomes before they ever happen. The customary view of accountability recognizes that people can gain more from a reactive strategy. The current view recognizes the opposite: people can achieve more from a proactive posture. This is because we believe that accountability is a broader concept than simply taking responsibility – it is something you do to yourself, not something that someone does to you.

It is with this version of accountability that people not only take accountability for the results they need to achieve individually, but become determined protectors of The Alliance shield and valued ambassadors of the entire organization. It is not hard to see why this prevailing notion of accountability (it is everyone's job) needs to be implemented in most organizations. Adopt this mindset and you will quickly realize that accountability is non-negotiable. It allows you to walk with dignity and avoid the creation of silos/cliques, finger pointing, and the blame game. Leonardo da Vinci wrote, "He who cannot establish dominion over himself will have no dominion over others."

Be A Self-Starter

BE SELF-DISCIPLINED

TAKE OWNERSHIP OF YOUR CHOICES

THINK BEFORE YOU ACT

BE A SELF-STARTER

Everyone wants to be a leader. However, few are prepared to accept the accountability that goes with it. But you cannot have one without the other. They go hand in hand. When leading others, you must make the conscious choice to go beyond what you are individually responsible for; representing a sense of ownership, involvement, and engagement. By nature, these three are only accomplished by initiative.

Taking initiative is aided by embracing the idea of being a self-starter. A self-starter is recognized by two traits: being persistent (never giving up) and remaining curious (truly wanting to understand). These two traits remind you that something needs to be done, and getting started means taking the first step rather than waiting for someone else or a better time. Like you've heard before, the time is NOW! Right Now!!!

In order to take initiative, we have to push past our own excuses and insecurities. This requires an attitude of accountability, which gives us the permission to fill in the gaps of wasted time with functional, practical and useful steps to take back our lives. Aristotle wrote:, "I count him braver who overcomes his desires than him who overcomes his enemies, for the hardest victory is victory over self."

respect

VALIDATION
BUILDING SELF-WORTH

▶ EMPATHY ▶ UNDERSTANDING

COURTESY
DISPLAYING POLITENESS

▶ MANNERS ▶ CIVILITY

DIPLOMACY
DEMONSTRATING TACTFULNESS

▶ PROFESSIONALISM ▶ HUMILITY

chapter 5

THE ALLIANCE PLAYBOOK DEFINITION OF

respect

"PROMOTING AN ENVIRONMENT WHERE BEING COURTEOUS, HELPFUL, AND DIVERSITY IS VALUED."

Respect is when **Civility** (displaying politeness) meets **Humility** (demonstrating tactfulness). Respect conveys a sense of admiration through a helpful spirit by exhibiting Care (validation with empathy); Consideration (courtesy with manners); and Concern (diplomacy with professionalism).

respect

VALIDATION
BUILDING SELF-WORTH

+

COURTESY
DISPLAYING POLITENESS

+

DIPLOMACY
DEMONSTRATING TACTFULNESS

Our fifth core value or pillar that holds up the House of The Alliance is Respect. In order to exhibit respect within The Alliance House, one must accept the following formula: Validation + Courtesy + Diplomacy. The Alliance measures validation by building self-worth; courtesy by displaying politeness; and diplomacy by demonstrating tactfulness.

albright's answers on respect

"My life is my message."
— Gandhi

Merriam-Webster dictionary: Respect: to consider worthy of high regard, or an act of giving particular attention.

Respect is a quality or trait that starts inside of you. When you have the proper amount of self-respect, then you are able to extend the same courtesy to those inside your circle and even people you don't know.

The amount of respect you show to others speaks volumes about how much you value that person. It is really an evaluation you are attaching to a person. There are several factors that come into play when dealing with the level of respect you show people.

Some ways we gauge the respect we show others is based on the following:

-Are they honest?
-Are they considerate of others?
-Are they responsible?
-Are they caring and understanding of others?
-Are they goal oriented?

One historical figure that showed great respect to other people is Mahatma Gandhi (Oct. 2, 1869-Jan. 30, 1948). He preached non-violence at a time when many cultures were being beyond violent toward those with opposing views. Gandhi used a simple list of 10 rules he believed could help a single person change the world for the better.

Gandhi's 10 Rules To Change The World

- Change yourself
- You are in control
- Forgive and let it go
- Without action, you aren't going anywhere
- Take care of this moment
- Everyone is human
- Persist
- See the good in people and help them
- Be congruent, be authentic, be your true self
- Continue to grow and evolve

Gandhi was born and raised in a Hindu merchant family in coastal Gujarat, India. He trained in law at the Inner Temple, and first employed non-violent civil disobedience as an expatriate lawyer in South Africa. He returned to India in 1915 and started protesting with farmers and laborers against excessive land-taxes and discrimination. In 1921, Gandhi assumed leadership of the Indian National Congress and led nationwide campaigns for social causes.

Gandhi led Indians in challenging British-imposed salt taxes in 1930, and eventually was imprisoned for years in South Africa and India for leading these movements. Gandhi lived modestly in a residential community and wore the traditional Indian dhoti and shawl, with a hand-spun charkha. His diet was simple vegetarian food, and he went on long fasts as a way of self-purification and political protest.

Gandhi continued pushing for India's independence well into the 1940s. Eventually, Britain granted independence, but the British Indian Empire was split into two dominions – a Hindu-majority India and Muslim-majority Pakistan. With many displaced Hindus, Muslims and Sokhs finding their way to new lands, religious violence broke out. Gandhi visited these areas, attempting to keep things peaceful. Gandhi went on several fasts in an effort to stop religious violence at the age of 78.

Some thought Gandhi was too accommodating toward India and the lack of payment it gave to Pakistan, which led to a Hindu nationalist assassinating Gandhi in 1948.

Gandhi dedicated his life to discovering the searching for truth, or Satya. His teachings and beliefs were adopted globally by other movements, including Martin Luther King, Jr.

Gandhi navigated the independence movement in the 1930-40s by speaking softly, standing up to British colonialists with strong speeches and non-violent protests. He is often named among the 20th century's most important figures and is heavily revered in India as a father of the nation.

Gandhi practiced what he preached to the world. When he took a stand for or against something, he backed it up with his words and actions. He didn't sit on the sideline and watch. He treated those less fortunate than him with the same level of respect he gave world leaders at the time. All lives mattered to Gandhi, and he believed they all deserved to be respected too.

What if you were able to apply Gandhi's 10 Rules To Change The World in your life? Do you think the world would be a better place? Do you think the level of respect you show to people you encounter on a daily basis would be improved? Would you be a better person?

I encourage you to know that you can change yourself now. You have the control to be better each day. When you feel like a person hurts you, lies to you, or doesn't treat you fairly; can you quickly forgive, let go and move on in a positive direction?

Can you start taking action faster when you know it is time to do so? Without moving, you aren't going to get anywhere. Practice living in the moment, so that you are truly present when it comes to those in your environment. Make every effort to recognize that everyone is human and will make mistakes. Treat people fairly, and certainly the way in which you would like to be treated.

Be persistent in doing your very best each day, and give others the same respect you expect in return. Be willing to find the good in people, and not only focus on areas where improvement is necessary. Most people know they need to improve in certain areas, and they might not appreciate you pointing out their flaws. Instead, give people a little honey to offset the vinegar that is obvious to the world.

Believe in your heart that people have good inside them and help them bring it out for the world to see. People need encouragement and they will deliver on a bigger level if you encourage them and tell them you believe in them. They will be more likely to return the encouragement in your direction when you need it also. Keep growing as a person, as a leader and teammate. We all need to evolve as people because that is how you keep growing and changing. We are not where we should be today, but we can get to where we want to be if we keep working hard to change for the better.

All these simple steps can help you become better with people, and they will help make sure that you are treating people with the proper level of respect. Make it part of your daily routine to extend the utmost respect to people you encounter. You might be surprised at the response you get from those who are treated unfairly by most of the world around them.

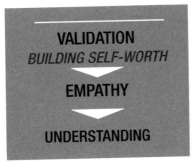

VALIDATION
BUILDING SELF-WORTH

EMPATHY

UNDERSTANDING

Let's now do a deep dive into the formula, starting with Validation. We claim that we want others to treat us with respect, and we need to show others respect. But what's the real meaning of this word? In the context of relating to the beliefs of others, the most basic and fitting definition is to have "due regard" for the other person's beliefs as they have for you.

"Due regard" means paying attention to another person's beliefs, but to "regard" something is to "look at it." The Latin origin of the word respect also means "to look back." Respect, therefore, is an observation. To respect a belief is to observe it and/or acknowledge its existence. So can you simply respect someone's beliefs by merely acknowledging that such beliefs exist?

The answer is no. You must follow up this acknowledgment or recognition of a belief with validation in order to show evidence of respect. Thomas Paine wrote "Give to every other human being every right that you claim for yourself." This is only accomplished through validating another's claim or truth. The process of making this vital connection with another human-being takes place in a sequential three step method:

1) Validation (Building self-worth): confirmation of another's internal experience which allows you to "break the ice" effectively.
2) Empathy (Considering the feeling): imagination on a moral track which allows you to "prime the pump" of someone's truth.
3) Understanding (Recognizing the feeling): installation of someone's frame of reference which allows you to "establish common ground."

Validating or step one is where you "chart the course" for where you want the relationship to go. Making statements like: "You are great," or "you bring value" helps disarm any hesitant participant. But be aware that if you are uncomfortable with intimacy, you may find validating others difficult because doing so brings you closer to them. People crave validation. Our perception of ourselves is inevitably shaped by the way others perceive and trust us. Validating words and actions builds a sense of self-worth. Using validation before attempting empathy greases the track and makes it much easier to connect to one another. Validation is like relationship glue.

Empathizing or step two is where you learn to "stay out of judgment." Making statements like: "I never thought of it that way," gives the listener the impression that you do not have to be right. Our best responses to the presence of others in our lives are born of "considering the feeling." Real empathy requires us to stay out of judgment and that's difficult if we are not self-aware. If we can't recognize the subtle, but more importantly, the differences between disappointment and anger in ourselves; it's virtually impossible to do it with others. Empathy isn't just about the vocabulary we use, but also about fully engaging with someone and wanting to consider their truth for a moment in time.

One of the greatest challenges we will face on this path to developing empathy is overcoming the need to be right and judging others. Shame, fear and anxiety are all major incubators of judgment. We mistakenly believe we can escape the pressure of these three by judging others. This need to evaluate others comes from our one need to compare our abilities, beliefs, and values against others. This need to compare can quickly turn into bias and prejudice if left unchecked. Prejudice is when you give your fears a name in the form of the unknown or what we don't understand.

Empathy doesn't condone or accept a said behavior, it just recognizes another's truth and considers why they feel the way they do. Empathy says to the other person that they have a right to their opinions. This is a vulnerable choice because it requires you to swallow your pride and leave your bias in the past.

Understanding or step three is when you practice what is called: "perspective taking." This technique is best represented in the En Vogue song from the 1990s: "Before you can read me, you must first learn how to see me." Making statements like: "Tell me more," invites the listener to express their views, which solidifies that they and their opinions count.

Our survival as a society and your success as a human being depends upon our ability to accurately understand and sensitively respond to each other. To mature is to gain a heartfelt understanding that others have value and are entitled to respect and consideration. This perspective will make it easier for you to say or do something meaningful. You want to show people that you value time spent with them.

In order to be empathetic, we must be willing to follow up the consideration state with the recognition and acknowledgment of the situation by experiencing through another's lens. You must work hard not to see their stories through your own lens. This is called "perspective taking," or seeing the world through multiple lenses. Recognizing others' perspective as their truth is the key ingredient to empathy and gives birth to allowing the establishment of common ground (understanding).

VALIDATION

"Kind words can be short and easy to speak but their echoes are truly endless."

- Mother Teresa

Moral: Confirmation of the long-lasting effects of another's words.

EMPATHY

"I do not ask the wounded person how he feels, I myself must become the wounded person."

- Walt Whitman

Moral: Consider what they feel.

UNDERSTANDING

"To perceive is to suffer."

- Aristotle

Moral: Recognize the why they feel.

albright's answers on validation

Validation is one way that we communicate acceptance of ourselves and others. Validation doesn't mean agreeing or approving. When your best friend or a family member makes a decision that you really don't think is wise, validation is a way of supporting them and strengthening the relationship while maintaining a different opinion. Validation is a way of communicating that the relationship is important and solid even when you disagree on issues.

Validation is the recognition and acceptance of another person's thoughts, feelings, sensations, and behaviors as understandable. In order for this recognition and accepting to take place, you must first quit trying to decide if you agree with them before you can validate them. Stop shutting people down and start making them feel safe so that they will begin leaning toward you.

Validation is also about the inflection of your vocabulary. There is a genuine concern "wow" and a sarcastic "wow" for example. It is important to stay clear of judgment with your words by not projecting an evaluating nature. This strategy tends to disarm people. Does this scripting of validation make you a fake? If you take a shower, does that make you a fake person also? The shower disguises that you were dirty before. Most people shower daily and that's good. It's the same as knowing what to say when you are on the phone or talking to people in person. You practice to the point where it becomes a habit. You are prepared because you have done it so often. When you practice a rehearsed validation, empathy and understanding, you are being a courteous and diplomatic leader. You are demonstrating respect for another human-being.

It turns out that humans have a need to belong and feel accepted whether they are happy or sad. It has a calming influence. Life can be confusing and difficult at times, but the proper validation lets us know that we are normal and gives us social confirmation that we bring value. Knowing that you are heard and understood is a powerful experience and one that seems to relieve labels. When we don't feel understood, it creates thoughts of being left out or not fitting in. Whatever the reason, validation helps soothe the emotional upset and helps them feel they deserve better.

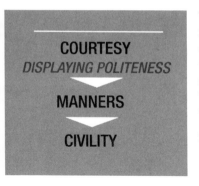

COURTESY
DISPLAYING POLITENESS

MANNERS

CIVILITY

The second part of the formula for Respect is Courtesy. First we must clear up a difficult distinction between the word "polite" and the word "courteous." Politeness is almost a ritual response like saying "please" and "thank you." While "courteous" is more of an upbringing, a refinement or graciousness that gives birth to polite behavior. This upbringing or refinement comes from being taught "manners." It is an attitude which instills a belief (etiquette and decorum) that is essential in civilized society.

The enemy of a "courteous nature" is the concept of "rudeness." Rudeness is the face of disrespect and is a weak person's imitation of strength. To be unable or unwilling to align one's behavior with the norms known to the general population, is to be considered "rude" and not socially acceptable. There are two types of rudeness:

1) Unfocused rudeness; not directed to anyone special and delivered without malice. Example: showing up to a HotSpot late.

2) Focused rudeness; directed at someone with malice. Example: targeting the leader of a HotSpot while he/she shows the plan with questions outside the scope of the script.

In order to avoid being considered "rude," one must start behaving in a way that benefits others. This is the very essence of "courtesy" -- considering the effect of your behavior. But the precursor to such behavior is accepting the customs and following the rules that govern that behavior. Manners have to become the reason that causes you to behave a certain way. Your manner is how you must behave, regardless of cause and effect.

Manners have been called "the shadows of our virtues." They are useful guides in the performances of our duties. They teach us to conduct ourselves appropriately with a well-cultured behavior due to a belief in prevailing customs and traditions. Manners/etiquette is a way to pay reverence to existing and accepted social standards of decency. Both manners and etiquette are codes of conduct that are sometimes linked with the word, "morals." Manners are the first step to morality and etiquette is the first gesture of ethics.

Manners cease to have meaning without morals and etiquette ceases to exist without them. Good manners are the rules of etiquette and good morals means one has the integrity to obey the rules. The enemy of manners and etiquette is "disrespect." Disrespect comes in two forms:

1) Arrogance (which is the root of "unfocused rudeness"). It manifests itself as disregard or distain which causes the "unworthy" tag for another human-being. Therefore, prompting the turning of a blind eye with a clear conscious.

2) Hate (which is the root of "focused rudeness"). It manifests itself as contempt or scorn which causes one to believe someone or something is "worthless" or despicable; thereby, prompting a negative reaction.

In order to combat such offensive "disrespect," one cannot just apply the rules of etiquette or rely on the decorum established by good manners. Instead, first develop an attitude that acknowledges the human rights of others to live together in a way where all parties refrain from harming one another. This attitude is evident by the "choice" we make every day on how we are going to behave. This simply means we have a "choice" to opt for "civility." It will come from valuing our differences and watching our tongues.

Civility comes from the word "civilis," which in Latin means "citizen." The way to measure your citizenship is to look at the quality of your response to the membership of society, community, or organization. It is our obligation or civic duty to this thing called: "The Collective We." This notion of civility suggests robust, even passionate, engagement framed in the respect of differing opinions and diverse belief systems.

Civility has to mean something more than mere "politeness." Its meaning is lost if all it accomplishes is to get people to say, "excuse me." It must create an environment of constructive confrontation, a safe place where its members do not have to walk on eggshells. A place where differing views promote synergy (from the greek word "synergia" which means, "working together") instead of creating separation in the form of cliques.

COURTESY

"We must be as courteous to a man as we are to a good picture, which we are willing to give advantage of good light."

- Ralph Waldo Emerson

Moral: Being polite gives people the benefit of the doubt.

MANNERS

"Respect for ourselves guides our morals; respect for others guides our manners."

- Lawrence Sterne

Moral: Respect for self is necessary for a civil servant to not accept a bribe when chances of getting caught is zero. Therefore, our manners are contingent on what we think we are.

CIVILITY

"Being civil means being constantly aware of others and weaving restraint and respect into the very fabric of this awareness."

- P.M. Forni

Moral: Keep your poise (learning when to walk away) as well as be assertive (actively promoting an environment where all individuals feel safe and supported).

albright's answers on courtesy

Common courtesy and general respect are things we need to show everyone. It should not merely be something we choose to reserve for a select few who we feel deserve it. Acting respectful around others requires manners and respectfulness. We demonstrate civility and separate ourselves from wild beasts by asserting self-control over our rudeness. It takes great strength, at times, to be civil to others.

The best way to deal with disrespectful people is to show them respect. Showing them disrespect in return will only lower ourselves to their level as well as give them additional reasons to continue to disrespect us. Most people will admire the courtesy that they are being shown and gradually change their attitude toward us.

Rude is the poor man's imitation of power. People do business with people they like. HotSpots are growing where the people are genuinely courteous. They are not blatantly blowing smoke, but rather just serving others. Courteous people will be judged on their acts. Likeability is created by politeness. The condition of civility provides an attitude of manners which causes this behavior of politeness.

Manners are just the shadows cast from courteous behaviors. People may not always remember the polite action, but will recall the manners you leave behind. At the root of manners is your belief in civility. Coaching your team without arrogance or an agenda is not possible without being civil. Allowing civility to be the master of your value system gives permission for a well-mannered demeanor to take hold of your personality, which is reflected in a polite delivery.

However, one does not have to be truly respectful of another to be courteous. This is because being courteous does not require admiration for the individual, it merely promotes polite social interaction which is evidence of etiquette from a civilized person.

Unlike, in this case of courtesy, where we become polite for almost anyone, respect does not function in that manner. Respect comes from within us as we view the positive aspects and the amazing traits of other people. It is these traits that makes us respect them. When we are courteous, we are not bothered about the character, qualities or achievements of the individual; but with respect, it is these features that make us admire and honor that individual. This is the main difference between courtesy and respect.

DIPLOMACY

DEMONSTRATING TACTFULNESS

PROFESSIONALISM

HUMILITY

The third part of the formula for Respect is Diplomacy. It is the established method of influencing through dialogue and negotiation tactics. In order to take this best course of action, one must remain poised by being tactful, and not reacting with negative rhetoric. By choosing your words carefully and always knowing your audience before delivering a message, you are demonstrating the highest degree of respect. As the English Proverb warns: "To talk without thinking is to shoot without aiming."

If being open to new ideas is difficult for you, then practicing diplomacy and being mindful before speaking will be equally difficult for you. Diplomacy is an art form for dealing with people in a sensitive and effective way. The ability to communicate with diplomacy is a skill that all agents, professionals and business owners need to master. Giving everyone you speak with the benefit of the doubt and cushioning your differing opinions with unemotional attachments is the best proof of your ability to provide others with a "diplomatic nature."

If diplomacy is a tactful behavior, "professionalism" is about the attitude behind behavior. This attitude allows one to perform at a consistent and higher level, while, at the same time, creating and maintaining the respect one seeks from colleagues and clients. Your attitude, while working, can determine the quality of your professional relationships, affect your productivity level, and cause an internal habit of work that will bleed into your private life.

Displaying a positive professional attitude requires you to think about and decide how you want to be perceived by others. Therefore, professionalism is an attitude adjustment aligned with an image makeover. This new image helps portray the perception that you might be more responsible, more diplomatic, and more mature. Basically professionalism is made up of three ingredients:

1. Work Ethic (punctual and shows up ready to work) - responsible.
2. Integrity (follows instruction and is perceived as representative of the organization) - diplomatic.
3. Self-motivation (self-starter and an opportunity seeker) - mature

Finally, it is the virtue of "Humility" that will lead our lives to the greatness found in learning how to be a professional. A person without humility risks intoxication by their own perceived importance. True professionalism, the kind needed throughout our lives, will only be found in those rare individuals that seek wise council, admit when they are wrong, and allow others to take the credit for success. Diplomacy, Professionalism, and Humility are the characteristics that empower our ability to serve and show respect. All three make a significant contribution when developing leadership qualities in an individual, but is the quality of humility that moves you from good to great.

Humility or humbleness is a condition that demands us to be respectful of others. It is the opposite of "boastfulness" and "vanity." Rather than a "me first" attitude, it requires a "team-first" attitude. Humility allows us to see the dignity and worth of having a professional attitude, and promoting a more diplomatic stategy when trying to connect people to each other and the ideals that govern us.

This humble demeanor cannot be practiced through arrogance and anger. We must respect all of our fellow human-beings. Humility comes with the knowledge that "Love Conquers All" and transcends our own narrow interests. True wealth is only realized by humility and by the honoring of others. It may be too easily dismissed as a leadership quality because people associate it with weakness.

However, according to several leadership experts, humility simply means understanding your strengths, weaknesses, and recognizing the strengths and weaknesses of others. Humble leaders are focused on the big picture of mission and team rather than themselves. This is best represented with the lyrics in the song "Ben" by Michael Jackson: "It used to be about I and me, but now it's us, now it's we."

True humility also requires courage and trust that stems from the leader's confidence in themselves and their abilities. Leaders that demonstrate humility hold people accountable, have tough conversations, and make difficult choices. They role-model, promoting a bigger purpose above the self-seeking approach. Those are the kinds of leaders that people follow.

DIPLOMACY

"Tact is the art of making a point without making an enemy."

- Isaac Newton

Moral: There are always two sides when making a point. Therefore, being absolute is the enemy of becoming tactful.

PROFESSIONAL

"A professional is someone who can do his best when he doesn't feel like it."

- Alistair Cooke

Moral: In contrast, the unprofessional is one who can't when they do feel like it.

HUMILITY

"But the greatest among you shall be your servant. And whoever exalts himself shall be humbled, and whoever humbles himself shall be exalted."

- Matthew 23:11-12

Moral: Agents should focus on the fraternal spirit and unity of the team.

albright's answers on diplomacy

Thomas Paine once wrote, "Character is much easier kept than recovered." Diplomacy is the answer to protecting your character. A diplomatic person is one that can be three things: 1) sensitive when dealing with others; 2) facilitate discussion; and 3) achieve resolutions of compromise. Responding with diplomacy and grace helps you master the act of being tactful. Practicing diplomacy is necessary in order to handle sensitive people.

Sensitivity is a form of judgment. This sensitivity on the part of others can cause them to dissect everything you say. It will require you to handle them with kid gloves or to be diplomatic. Using tact and diplomacy appropriately can lead to improved relationships with other people and is a way to build and develop mutual respect; which in turn can lead to more successful outcomes and less difficult or stressful communications with sensitive individuals.

Diplomacy comes from a professional attitude. This attitude is best explained for me this way: I did not like being broke. I hated it. So, I showed my respect everyday by being professional, by being competent, by being on fire. My professional attitude is evidence of a humble spirit. The acquisition of material wealth for me is just symbols of my willingness to stay humble and do the work. Humility is what lets us go all the way to meet our goals, and thereby, giving us choice to meet the needs of others.

Acting with humility does not in any way whatsoever deny our own self-worth. After all, having a low opinion of one's self is not humility; it is self-destruction. Humility, instead, affirms the worth of every single person on the planet. We will gain more from being humble than we will ever sacrifice. Humility allows us to be respectful of others. It drives out arrogance, boastfulness, vanity and aggressiveness, and allows, as an alternative, a professional (business-like) demeanor.

Crises are inevitable. When the unexpected happens, you should strive to be remembered as the calm person in the room. Think about it -- would you rather have someone who can push through a crisis in a professional manner or one who freaks out? You make a choice to have a good attitude or a bad attitude. Your choice will affect your professionalism. If you consistently deliver top-quality work, you will get the kudos you deserve without resorting to self-promotion. Sharing the credit will win you loyalty points with your peers. The best way to sum up this discussion is with a Rick Warren quote, "humility is not thinking less of yourself, it is thinking of yourself less."

THE 4 BEHAVIORS OF

respect

BE TOLERANT AND ACCEPTING   **RELY ON THE FACTS**

BE CONSIDERATE   **SHOW HUMILITY**

On a practical level respect includes taking someone's feelings, needs, thoughts, ideas, wishes and preferences into consideration. It means taking all of these seriously and giving them worth and value. Respect can be shown through behavior, and it can also be felt. We can act in ways which are considered respectful, yet we can also feel respect for someone and feel respected by someone. But when the feeling is there, the behavior will naturally follow.

When we are respected, we gain the voluntary cooperation of people. We don't have to use as much of our energy and resources to get our needs met. Real respect is something that is earned over time. It seems to be like a boomerang in the sense that you must send it out before it will come back to you. Just remember: respect cannot be demanded or forced, though sometimes leaders mistakenly believe that it can. Respect is earned.

It seems that authority has two basic sources: fear and respect. Dysfunctional organizations base their leadership on fear because they do not have the patience to wait on respect. Waiting, however, creates a safe and inviting environment; where you are more likely to get honest answers and effective feedback.

In this type environment, respect takes three forms:
- Respect for myself
- Respect for others
- Respect for a belief system

Respect for myself: If we don't respect and love ourselves, it is very hard to respect and love others. It is important for us to develop the right heart toward others. When we show disrespect toward someone, what we are really saying is, "I do not think much of myself."

Respect for others: Respecting others requires that we treat all human beings – even those we may not favor – as having dignity, rights and value equal to our own. That is the essence of the Golden Rule: "Treat others as you want to be treated."

Respect for a belief system: We become complete human beings when we discover respect for something bigger than ourselves. Protecting the shield of The Alliance is our chance to honor the place we call home.

"To be one, to be united is a great thing. But to respect the right to be different is maybe even greater."

– Bono of U2

Moral: One of the best ways to show respect for someone is to truly listen and hear another's point of view. We should allow each other to have and express our own views - regardless of whether we agree with them or not.

Be Tolerant and Accepting

Tolerance is a fair and objective attitude toward those whose opinions and practices differ from one's own, which produces a commitment to respect human dignity. It has been proven that tolerating differing opinions actually strengthens an organization or society, as evidenced by the growth of democracies over the past several hundred years.

One of the ways we can develop and deepen our respect, tolerance and be more accepting of other people, is through empathy. It is a way for us to try to understand where they are coming from and to see the world through their eyes. There is a wise old saying: "Do not judge another person until you have walked a mile in their shoes." Learning to empathize is not easy. It may be the hardest human emotion known to humankind. It is a challenge to our heart to grow and extend itself out to embrace others. By making this emotional connection with them, we can avoid destructive conflict and negative feelings, which in turn, creates respect. Empathy leads us to ask ourselves, "If I were in that person's situation, how would I want to be treated?" Treatment is the connecting bridge between empathy and respect.

"Tolerance isn't about not having beliefs. It's about how your beliefs lead you to treat people who disagree with you." - Timothy Keller

Treatment is the connecting bridge between empathy and respect.

Be Considerate

BE TOLERANT AND ACCEPTING

RELY ON THE FACTS

BE CONSIDERATE

SHOW HUMILITY

Courtesy and good manners enable people to get along with each other and resolve problems in a peaceful way. People, however, can observe rude behaviors in others, but cannot recognize their own inconvenient actions. Sometimes emotions take over, or we may have bad habits that we've been blinded by through the years.

So, what does it mean to be mannerly? It means that the person is warm and genuine, with a commitment to being considerate and kind to others. It also means having the awareness not to inconvenience others with your own junk. Thinking and acting like the world owes you something, believing that there are two sets of rules: the rules for you and the rules for everybody else – will kill any respect that you may wish to gain from anyone.

A person of great manners uses tact, values honesty and understands the power of words and actions. As you grow in etiquette (displaying impeccable manners) remember not to allow your biases and opinions to draw you away into vain and corrupting conversations. Someone who knows proper etiquette deals with awkward situations with grace and poise. You see, good manners are a visible sign that you as a person are polished and professional. You can act out of respect as well as being considerate and caring (an act of kindness).

Rely on the Facts

BE TOLERANT AND ACCEPTING

BE CONSIDERATE

RELY ON THE FACTS

SHOW HUMILITY

Facts and proper critical analysis will give you a framework that can help you understand yourself and the outside world. Using facts as a foundation by which you understand reality will help you to identify, acknowledge, and accept that you have good and bad attributes. Having a foundation will help you recognize and reconcile with the fact that you have negative attributes, which are blocking you from succeeding in your endeavors. Facts will also help shut down rationalizations that support your inflated ego.

Rationalizing is a protection mechanism for your ego, and it will occur even when the rationalization causes you to have unproductive motives that are damaging to your ability to earn respect from others. We have all heard, "The truth hurts." Well, in order to hear the truth, we must reconcile with our ego and stop rationalizations (which are based on assumptions), and know that there is always room for improvement. This improvement should be founded on the facts and not what we want the truth to be.

No one always acts purely objectively and rationally. We often connive for selfish interests. We gossip, boast and exaggerate about the truth. It is only human to wish to validate our prior knowledge, to vindicate our prior decisions, or to sustain our earlier beliefs. In this process of satisfying our ego, however, we can often deny ourselves intellectual growth and opportunity. We may not always want to apply the facts, but if we want to have respect for ourselves as well for others, then we must rely on reason rather than emotion. We must weigh the influences of motives and biases, and recognize our own assumptions, prejudices or points of view.

Show Humility

BE TOLERANT AND ACCEPTING

RELY ON THE FACTS

BE CONSIDERATE

SHOW HUMILITY

Humility is a way of behaving, and we must be intentional about practicing it. In order to adopt the habits and heavier patterns of humility, it's important to recognize its evil nemesis – ARROGANCE! Very few things damage one's reputation quicker than arrogance. Remember, arrogance is an attitude where people believe they are superior to everyone else.

For example, arrogant people often push others aside because they believe they are the only ones qualified to get things done the right way; they speak in ways that put down or disparage others; they take every opportunity to boast about their own accomplishments; and they project an obvious air of trying to appear cool.

There is only one reason that people are afflicted with this disease of arrogance and it is simply this: pride. Pride is one of, if not the greatest, trap that has snagged many great and talented leaders. It is still catching egos today. Seriously, imagine if adults had the humility to say "sorry," or even the humility to say, "I was wrong." Humility, not pride, makes everyone more teachable and more reachable.

We have all heard that "pride comes before the fall," but do we believe it? The most effective way to achieve the great virtue of humility is humiliation. So don't be afraid to fall. Being humiliated is humbling and essential for anyone trying to change the world, for it makes us better listeners.
The good news is that you don't have to sacrifice self-confidence to practice humility. When we start to talk about humility, one of the primary objections of driven people is fear of not appearing confident enough. I will assure you that adopting this practice does not require you to sacrifice your dignity.

To clarify this, let's look at the definitions of both confidence and humility.

CONFIDENCE: a self-assurance arising from an appreciation of one's true abilities.

HUMILITY: having a modest opinion or estimate of one's own importance or rank. It's about being open to the possibility of improvement.

There's no reason why these two character traits can't co-exist. In fact, when they do, it's hard to find a more powerful combination. The two working together in concert keep you from gloating about your latest superstar, but rather keep you going to find even more superstars.

By its very nature, humility is not an attitude we ever perfect. It's a practical trait that requires constant monitoring, especially since arrogance is always tugging at our human nature.

Nobel Peace Prize winner Rabindranath Tagore describes both the benefits and practice of humility well. He says, "We come nearest to great when we are great in humility." When you practice humility, you gain the respect of others. Respect brings with it a number of rewards such as more satisfying relationships, broader influence and increased productivity.

compassion

NOTICING
APPLYING CREDENCE

▶ FAITH

▶ CONVICTION

CONNECTING
PRACTICING LOVE

▶ ATTRACTION

──────────────▶ AFFECTION

▶ ADMIRATION

RESPONDING
CONVEYING SYMPATHY

▶ TOGETHER FEELING

▶ FELLOW FEELING

chapter

THE ALLIANCE PLAYBOOK DEFINITION OF

compassion

"DISPLAYING URGENCY WHEN DEALING WITH DISTRESS AND ADVOCATING EMPATHY FOR FELLOW AGENTS AND STAFF"

Compassion is when becoming **Responsive** (sympathy-driven urgency) meets **Noticing** (empathy-driven concern). This compassionate connection explains how we can strengthen our bonds with others.

compassion

NOTICING
APPLYING CREDENCE

CONNECTING
PRACTICING LOVE

RESPONDING
CONVEYING SYMPATHY

Our sixth core value or pillar that holds up the House of The Alliance is Compassion. In order to demonstrate compassion with The Alliance House, one must accept the following formula: **Noticing + Connecting + Responding.** The Alliance measures noticing by applying credence; connecting by practicing love; and responding by conveying sympathy.

albright's answers on compassion

Merriam-Webster definition of Compassion: sympathetic consciousness of others' distress together with a desire to alleviate it.

If you are under the age of 40, there's a good chance you don't know who Fred Rogers was. For millions of adults in the United States, he was the model example of what is means to be compassionate as a human being. He believed that every person was important to the world and that they deserved to be loved for being exactly who they are.

A new generation of people were introduced to Fred Rogers in the 2018 documentary, "Won't You Be My Neighbor?" Additionally, Tom Hanks stars as Fred Rogers in a movie about the man many of us grew up calling Mr. Rogers. His show, "Mr. Rogers Neighborhood" started at a local affiliate television station in Pittsburgh and grew into a national hit on the PBS channel.

Fred Rogers introduced characters on the show that taught young people life lessons about how we should behave, interact with and, ultimately, treat people in our life. He tackled social issues at a time when it was taboo to even touch those subjects in terms of race, sexuality and social issues. Rogers was miles ahead of society when it came to being open-minded to people who were considered "different" than what was popular or normal in the 1960s, 70s and 80s.

There's a perfectly good reason why both a movie and a documentary are being made about Fred Rogers' life. He was a good man, who believed in being good to people because it was the right thing to do, and we are living in a time when people need to hear his message of compassion over and over again. He taught children how to treat others through his TV show, and he impacted millions of young people in a way that they never forgot. He is the definition of what it means to exercise compassion.

Many people believe our nation is divided right now. There are school shootings, hate-filled newscasts and people would almost rather engage in personal attacks than to have a rational disagreement. The world can be an ugly place these days.

With that being said, I don't think the world has to be so complicated. What if we all focused on showing more love, empathy, understanding and compassion to people on a daily basis? What if we all were better "neighbors" like in the world Mr. Rogers created on his TV show?

One of Mr. Rogers' popular songs was titled, "It's a Beautiful Day in the Neighborhood." What if we treated people in such a manner that they truly felt like life in their little world was more beautiful? People don't always remember what you say to them, but they certainly remember exactly how you made them feel!

Most of what Fred Rogers did on his TV show was unorthodox in terms of best TV practices, but it worked because of the positive messages and stories he was able to tell through puppets and odd set designs in his studio. I loved the positivity he provided to children. He let them each know they were special in their own way. He encouraged them to be true to who they were and to like people for who they were inside and not for the way they looked or the possessions they owned. Mr. Rogers did not judge others.

Even though he died in 2003, people still look to Mr. Rogers as a voice of reason in an extremely noisy world. In times of trouble, Fred Rogers' mother told him, "Always look for the helpers during times of crisis. There are always helpers. If you look for the helpers, you will know that there is hope."

I want to be a helper for people who are in need. I want you to do the same. Mr. Rogers had a calming presence and kind demeanor. I wouldn't mind being his neighbor, how about you?

Even when other people were criticizing Rogers as being fake or strange, he rose about the critics and continued providing a positive example for the world to see. I would like to be more like Mr. Rogers as a person. He chose to exercise compassion all the time, not just when it was easy. He was consistent. Mr. Rogers was patient, kind, genuine, loving, helpful, inclusive, gentle, accepting, imaginative, curious and, most of all, compassionate.

I'm trying to practice more of the qualities that made Mr. Rogers great, specifically compassion. I'm doing my best to find the positive in situations rather than focusing or complaining about issues when they pop up. I seek solutions to problems instead of belittling people with struggles, challenges or problems. I do my best to keep my efforts focused on what is in front of me and not what is behind and in the past. In all situations, I'm working to find ways to include everybody on my team so they feel important. Nobody likes feeling left out.

If we could all be a little bit more like Mr. Rogers, our "neighborhood" would be better, and we would all be better people too. I encourage you to find ways to show more compassion toward people in your life. It will make you a better person, and people will remember how you made them feel.

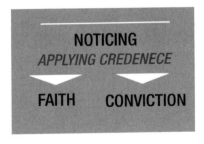

Let's now do a deep dive into the formula, starting with Noticing.

First, Compassion is the effort of trying to relieve the pain of others. This effort comes from a concern for the well-being of others.

In the classical teachings of the Buddhist tradition, compassion is defined as the heart that trembles in the face of suffering. It is aspired as the noblest quality of the human heart, even for those who have intentionally transgressed. Compassion is the acknowledgement that not all pain can be fixed or solved, but all suffering is made more approachable in a landscape of caring.

Above all, compassion is the capacity to open your heart to the reality of suffering and aspire to its healing. It is this response to a specific subjective feeling which tugs on the heart strings of forgiveness.

Compassion comes into the English language by way of the Latin root "passio" which means to "suffer," paired with the Latin prefix "com" meaning "together" -- to suffer together. It involves "connection" to others and "caring" for those others. It involves a focus on the other and a desire for the other to have good things happen or to overcome adversity. It is the exploring of the process of noticing, connecting and responding.

Noticing is the practice of being mindful. Whenever we do this with another's problems, we align ourselves with their pains, and thereby, give said pains "credence." By giving someone or something credence, we are just one small step away from believing it to be true. Compassion is a way of giving credit to another's thought; as the Latin root word "cred" means "believe."

However, consciously or unconsciously, with every interaction, we are all making the choice to build our compassion credit or empty it out. We are all the keepers of our own compassion accounts. If someone drains our account dry, we are not obligated to keep offering them credit. Thereby, our faith in them and convictions for them become weakened.

Rick Warren writes: "kindness always starts with noticing the needs and hurts of others." But to apply credence to such need and hurt with first noticing, one must possess "faith" (overcoming excuses not to) and "conviction" (overcoming easons not to).

Many use the terms "Faith" and "Conviction" interchangeably, when really they are two entirely different concepts. Faith requires not knowing for sure, in an empirical way, that something is true. Conviction, on the other hand, requires the exact opposite. The word conviction comes from the verb, "to be convinced." In order to be convinced of something, there has to be observed facts from which the conviction has been derived. In other words, it is easier to "notice" and give credence with faith behind it, rather than with conviction behind it. But in order to turn that noticing into "connecting" and "responding," I must eventually appeal to a person's convictions.

If I am dealing with someone who has faith that something is so, then I tend to leave them to it. I'm simply not going to be able to persuade them of any other view, because their standard of proof is too low, and their defense barrier is too high. But if there is a point where someone's "belief" is based on a conviction (an interpretation of facts), it inevitably permits the opportunity of being changed.

However, convictions, that cause people to say: "It's the principle of the matter," -- are letting their beliefs interpret the facts instead of the facts influencing their beliefs. This twisted logic of wishing what they want to be true (blind faith) and judging based on a small sample size (witness-led convictions) is what is called in today's popular culture as the manufacturing of "fake news."

In summary, noticing is applying credence or believing in something you feel is real. But the precursors of "faith" or assurance (accepting of something you can't see) and "conviction" or reliance (depending on something you can see), are both needed to master the art of noticing.

FAITH

"Now he understood that roads do divide, at the crossroads there is a choice, and blinding oneself to it is a form of choosing too."

- Eric Christian Haugaard from "The Untold Tale"

Moral: Your faith can move mountains, but your blind faith can also create them.

CONVICTION

"Conviction is worthless unless it is converted into conduct."

- Thomas Carlyle

Moral: A strong conviction that is not acted upon, becomes the parent to many regrets to come.

albright's answers on noticing

For you to have compassion, you really must believe that you want others to succeed. You are not jealous of them. You do not wish bad things on them. You do not judge them off their past experiences. You do, rather, wish they could improve moving forward and wish good things to happen to them. That is the requirement of compassion: noticing others with faith (believe they can be better) and conviction (trying to help them get better).

In a psychological test done using monkeys in a cage, a scare thermometer was placed in each monkey with electrodes that monitors their stress levels. The first monkey is placed in a small cage alone. Within minutes he is shaking from being isolated away from the other monkeys being put in a strange new cage. A second monkey is introduced to the cage with the first monkey. The scare thermometer only registers half the level of isolation as found in the first monkey. Both monkeys being together creates less stress based on their anxiety levels. When they noticed each other, they begin to complement each other with comfort. This is the way people feel when you hire them, if you put them beside you, they will come along faster, which lessens their fears.

Another example of this would be watching a scary movie about a bad guy in the woods. The group is sitting around a campfire and somebody needs to go to the bathroom. You start to scream at the TV, "no, no – take someone with you." There is safety in numbers. If you put a third monkey in the small cage, the dynamics change entirely. They all three feed off each other's confidence and positive vibes and start to plot how to get out. They have gone from being scared to now: "We're a gang. We're going to win. We got this. We've got a shot."

The more people believe they are the same and in the same boat, getting out and trying to survive becomes their natural instinct. That is why HotSpots mean so much. It gives our business a way to connect with people and show their compassion by noticing. Compassion becomes a way of giving credit to another person's need to be valued. If you do not deliver this kind of compassion, people will not stay or come back. If you give them judgment over their wrinkly clothes, for example, or you ignore their very existence at the HotSpot, they will have a distain for our company. Call it compassion or call it kindness; either one works, but noticing is the first step. Noticing must become your conviction and shown in the form of conduct (action).

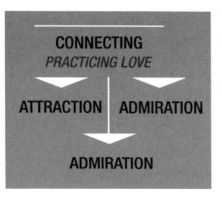

CONNECTING
PRACTICING LOVE

ATTRACTION   ADMIRATION

ADMIRATION

The second part of the formula for Compassion is Connecting. It is what we experience in any moment when we are with someone without our judgments about them or ourselves. Love, therefore, is complete, unconditional acceptance. Love doesn't require anything in return. It is about connecting without expectations.

There are two definitions for real, genuine love:

1)Love is when you choose to be at your best when the other person is not at their best (never keeping score).

2)Love is when what you want is never important. But what the other person needs and wants is always paramount (no norm of reciprocity is needed).

Love is when one person believes in another person and shows it with: desire, warmth and patience. Afterward, what we feel is reflected in what we do with the connection made. This connection comes in three forms or types of love: Eros, Agape, and Philos.

Eros is a Greek term which actually means desire and longing. According to the Bible, God created physical attraction, but never intended it to be selfish.

Agape is the love that God commanded all believers and non-believers to have for everyone in the form of affection. However, it should never be determined by our feelings; it is more of a set of behaviors or actions.

Philos is for a pal who is really close and dear to us, and it is characterized by various different experiences between two people. Philos is really wonderful but it is not very reliable, since it is dependent on the exchange between two unpredictable humans seeking fairness.

The following chart lists the three types of love, the cause and effect of each, and the gender-based want and eventual outcome due to their agendas:

1) **Attraction/Eros**: need-based kind of love
   (motivational, for example, by making money with passion).

Cause →	Effect →	Outcome/Want	
"Desire"	Temptation	(men) acknowledgement of the:	**TASK**
		(women) connection with the:	

2) **Affection/Agape**: giving kind of love
   (emotional, for example, by making difference with commitment).

Cause →	Effect →	Outcome/Want	
"Warmth"	Tenderness	(men) stability in their:	**SELF**
		(women) acceptance of their:	**WORTH**

3) **Attachment/Philos**: companionship kind of love
   (cognitive, for example, by having fun with purpose).

Cause →	Effect →	Outcome/Want	
"Patience"	Tolerence	(men) fairness of the:	**EXCHANGE**
		(women) decency in the:	

Each person individually defines what an exceptional connection means to them, but there is a basic definition that can apply to all people. An exceptional connection is a bundle of subjective feelings that come together to create a bond between people. Without this connection, the road to the three types of love are blocked.

To connect with someone or something means to have a shared perspective of the world, to feel as though the other person or group thinks at the same level as your view. This sort of connection transcends the physical limitations of the human body. When your mind connects with something bigger than yourself, you share a bond that connects you through an entirely different dimension. This kind of connection cannot be justified through materialistic means; instead, it is comprised of something entirely different: unexplainable energy you draw from the compassions for another human-being.

ATTRACTION

"The secret of attraction is to love yourself."

- Deepak Chopra

Moral: In order to attract others and success, you must walk with confidence and believe in yourself.

AFFECTION

"Affections is responsible for nine-tenths of whatever solid and durable happiness there is in our lives."

- C.S. Lewis

Moral: Human contact and the recognition of existence afterward, is what every individual is ultimately thirsty for.

ATTACHMENT

"The secret of happiness is to become attached without desiring."

- Author Unknown

Moral: When the mission becomes bigger than the rewards, that is when the attachment becomes a priority, and an integral key to one's success.

albright's answers on connecting

Your objective when connecting with others is to try to remain inside the circle of you (which is where you worry about being the best you), while at the same time, still loving on the people outside your circle (which is where you care about them, but don't worry about them). You do not get depressed when they are mad. You do not get down when they are upset. You do not blow up when they become confrontational. You do not pout when they become unreasonable. You do not stop working when they become demanding. Your life continues regardless of those people outside the circle of you. But you still show them love and continue moving on.

You do not have to respect their decisions, but you continually love the divine spark that is in them. Hurt people, hurt people. Depressed people, depress people. Selfish people are selfish. But all are still human-beings, thirsty for love. However, these conditions inhibit them from delivering love in return.

The key difference between love and respect is that while love is an affection felt toward another, respect is an admiration. One can respect a person even if they are not in love with that person. But I doubt, if you really love someone if the basic feel of respect is missing. But just because you say you love someone does not mean you will treat them well. Many people disrespect and mistreat despite the presence of love. People feel love for others on a daily basis. The issue is a lack of respect for others as well as a lack of thought behind one's love. As Lionel Richie sang in his song entitled, "Sweet Love": "Don't just put a little love in your heart, but rather, put a little heart in your love."

We all like to think of ourselves as loving people. Some of us even take pride in being a "nice" person or a "good" person. However, no matter how hard we try, assuming all three types of love (attraction, affection, and attachment) are unconditional is foolish and arrogant. Relationships need to be maintained and people need to know they are appreciated.

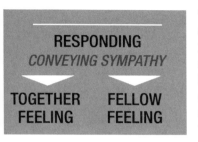

RESPONDING
CONVEYING SYMPATHY

TOGETHER   FELLOW
FEELING   FEELING

The third part of the formula for Compassion is Responding with sympathy. It is a feeling of care and concern for someone, often someone close, accompanied by a wish to see them better or happier. This active desire to alleviate the suffering of another is when sympathy attaches itself to the concept of compassion. With this connection, sympathy sheds its partial attitude and becomes more willing to give without expectations of reciprocity. As the Dalai Lama explains: "It is a necessity, not a luxury."

Responding requires a conscious decision to demonstrate condolences of pity and sorrow for someone else's misfortune. We may begin with *Apathy* (lack of attention or concern) for someone or something. Hopefully next, we may learn how to have *Sympathy* for the suffering of others. *Empathy* then moves us to feel with, to suffer with, and finally rejoice with others. From Empathy we can reach the ultimate spiritual step of *Compassion*. It is distinguished by its universality (compassion for all), and by the lack of panic or fear in it. Sympathy and Empathy, alone without a compassionate nature, and at a global level, are overwhelming to a jaded population. Compassion, however, when partnered with a tempered wisdom, has no problem reaching the larger masses. In this model of spiritual intelligence, I see no path to compassion without conveying sympathy first, then quickly following with empathy.

Cynics may dismiss compassion as irrational or misguided sentiment, but we know that people who help others are healthier, happier and live longer than those who don't. Compassion gets us out of the dumps – when our attention is on helping others, we get out of self, we begin to feel energized, and before we know it, we feel better. Depression has been linked to excessive self-focus, a preoccupation with "me, myself and I." But none of this is possible without being able to execute sympathy (willing to say what is expected of us). After these words of concern leave your mouth, your capacity to share an experience with another person through empathy is possible.

The Greek word for sympathy means (when broken down into two parts) sym: a "together feeling," and pathos: a "fellow feeling." In order to respond to another with sympathy, one must first experience this "together feeling" and "fellow feeling." Sympathy is a way of comforting people and demonstrating condolences for people.

Within the "together feeling" it's about creating what is called "interdependence." Having this together feeling says: "I'm dependent upon you, and you're dependent upon me." It is a "we're in it together" kind of thing. This together feeling is represented in two ways: 1) Spatial proximity (dependent on your preferences); and 2) Similar experiences (dependent on your relationships).

1) Spatial proximity is best explained by the division into two groups: In-groups (do identify with people that have similar beliefs); Out-groups (do not identify with people of differing beliefs). The secret to closing the spatial gap is getting outside your comfort zone (In-Group) by reaching across the aisle to the uncomfortable (Out-group). This is the only way you are going to grow as a person. Staying in your own little in-group, you are only going to hear their version of the truth, not the other version.

2) Similar experiences are best explained by the concept of "primary groups" vs "secondary groups." Primary groups are those that are close-knit and intimate, and are typically small in scale. Secondary groups are those that are more impersonal and temporary. The trick is to quickly move people from secondary status (acquaintances) to primary status (inner-circle). The hardest thing to do is building relationships with people that are different than you and making them feel like a part of the group.

In order to accomplish this, one must establish regular face-to-face or verbal interaction. In addition, one should also create a shared culture of common goals and encourage frequent engagement of activities together. The ties that bind the relationships of primary groups together are made up love, care, concern, loyalty and support.

RESPONDING

"How people treat you is their karma; how you react is yours."

- Wayne Dyer

Moral: How people treat you is their own deal; how you react to them is your deal. In Dyer's own words: "when you judge another, you do not define them, you define yourself."

SYMPATHY

"The role of friendship means there should be mutual sympathy between them, each supplying what the other lacks and trying to benefit the other, always using friendly and sincere words."

- Cicero

Moral: A true friend is not only your biggest critic and strongest supporter, but one that recognizes when you are vulnerable and need a sympathetic response in the spirit of Mr. Fred Rogers: "I like you just the way you are."

albright's answers on responding

Responding to another individual starts and ends with conveying sympathy. It is demonstrating a feeling of care and concern, accompanied by a wish to see somebody better off. Sympathy allows you to feel for them, while compassion lets you act on the feeling. Voltaire said, "tears are the silent language of grief." It is evidence that you care. Tears or tearing up is when you start to see somebody's real sympathy. Actively trying to relieve pain is when you show you care. When you marry action to desire, you are connecting compassion (taking action) to sympathy (desiring an outcome).

The key difference between sympathy and compassion is that sympathy means you can understand what another person is going through, whereas, compassion is the willingness to relieve the suffering of another. Thus, the degree of involvement indicates the difference between sympathy and compassion. The compassion indicates a higher degree of involvement than sympathy. But it is sympathy that must be the precursor to compassion. Both, however, are two words that indicate our reactions to the plight of others.

In order to provide compassion to others, we must first possess "self-compassion". It combines the skills of mindfulness (guarding your own endurance) with life satisfaction (living your life with purpose); which increases your emotional resilience and keeps you moving through the distractors, dysfunction, and distractions. It is motivated by the ancient and universal "golden rule" to treat others as you would like to be treated. Compassion will always have a measurable impact on the Alliance community and the members within our community.

THE 4 BEHAVIORS OF

compassion

NOTICE ANOTHER'S DISTRESS   RESPOND TO ANOTHER'S ANGUISH

CONNECT TO ANOTHER'S HURT   REPLENISH ANOTHER'S VOID

The basic nature of human beings is to be compassionate. The Biblical tradition, too, teaches compassion as a duty divine law, as a response to divine love, and a sign of commitment to the Judeo-Christian ethic. Compassion is a fundamental and timeless part of human existence.

Compassion is also an essential, yet often overlooked, aspect of life in organizations. Although organizations are frequently portrayed as sites of pain and suffering, they are also places of healing, where caring and compassion are both given and received.

Compassionate acts can be found at all levels in an organization, from leaders who buffer and transform the pain of their employees, to office workers, who listen and respond empathetically to their colleagues' troubles. Compassion in organizations makes people feel seen and known; it also helps them feel less alone.

"Consider how much your
actions will affect not only the
outcome, but also the journey of another."

– Author Unknown

*Moral: People need you along the path to
success more than they need you at the finish line.*

Notice Another's Distress

NOTICE ANOTHER'S DISTRESS	*RESPOND TO ANOTHER'S ANGUISH*
CONNECT TO ANOTHER'S HURT	*REPLENISH ANOTHER'S VOID*

A critical first step in the compassion process is noticing another person's suffering and becoming aware of the pain he or she is feeling. Noticing often requires openness and receptiveness to what is going on in those around us, paying attention to others' emotions, and reading subtle cues in our daily interactions with them.

People's motivation and skill in noticing varies across individuals and situations. We tend to find noticing easiest when the person is similar to us and when we like him or her. We are also more likely to detect a person's suffering when we have experienced a similar kind of pain ourselves. When we are especially busy at work and preoccupied with our own deadlines and concerns, we are often unable to notice the pain that may be in front of us. For that reason we must try to get out of the way of ourselves and see that everyone is experiencing hardships.

Connect to Another's Hurt

NOTICE ANOTHER'S DISTRESS   *RESPOND TO ANOTHER'S ANGUISH*

CONNECT TO ANOTHER'S HURT   *REPLENISH ANOTHER'S VOID*

Compassionate feelings resemble empathic concern in which a person imagines or feels the condition of the person in pain or suffering. Aristotle writes: "To perceive is to suffer." These feelings also involve taking the attitude of the other person, seeking the situation from their perspective, and taking the role of said person.

To feel empathic concern, we must, therefore, be able to appreciate the suffering person's pain from his or her perspective. The highest form of knowledge is empathy; for it requires us to suspend our egos and live in another's world. The most beautiful people are those who have known defeat, known suffering, known loss and have found their way out of the depths of hell. These persons have an appreciation, sensitivity, and an understanding of life that fills them with compassion, gentleness, gratitude, and a deep loving concern. You can't sing the blues if you have not lived the blues.

Respond To Another's Anguish

NOTICE ANOTHER'S DISTRESS   **RESPOND TO ANOTHER'S ANGUISH**

CONNECT TO ANOTHER'S HURT   REPLENISH ANOTHER'S VOID

In addition to connecting to those who suffer, the experience of compassion should also move those feeling the concern to act toward easing or eliminating the other's suffering. You see, compassion is not simply a sense of sympathy or caring for the person suffering, not simply a warmth of heart toward the person before you, or a sharp recognition of their needs and pain. It should produce a sustained and practical determination to do whatever is possible and necessary to help alleviate their suffering.

Compassionate responding may or may not be instrumental in fixing or correcting the immediate cause of one's suffering, but your action's aim should at least make the experience of the suffering more bearable. Feeling but not displaying compassion is still the net gain of doing nothing at all. When you feel connected to everything, you also feel responsible for everything. You, at that point, cannot turn away. Your destiny is now bound with the destinies of others. In the movie "Titanic," the main character Jack says to Rose, "You jump, I jump."

Caregiving emphasizes the enactment of a set of behaviors, such as inquiry, validation, and support. Furthermore, caregiving is seen as a way of replenishing a colleague who is emotionally drained or experiencing burnout from work.

Replenish Another's Void

NOTICE ANOTHER'S DISTRESS	*RESPOND TO ANOTHER'S ANGUISH*
CONNECT TO ANOTHER'S HURT	***REPLENISH ANOTHER'S VOID***

Just as the act of smiling has been found to generate positive affects in people, it also alerts others to the fact that the person engaging in the action is indeed feeling compassion. Although a feeling of compassion may have moral value in its own right, it is through compassionate responding that feeling comes to be a social force that compels interaction and promotes social solidarity.

When we honestly ask ourselves which people in our lives mean the most to us, we often find that it is those who (instead of giving advice, solutions, or cares) have chosen to first share in our pain, and who have chosen to touch our wounds with a warm and tender hand.

The friend who can be silent with us in a moment of despair or confusion, who can stay with us in an hour of grief and bereavement, who can tolerate not knowing the details; not curing or healing, but rather face with us the reality of powerlessness we all sometimes encounter in life - that is a friend who truly cares. Napoleon Hill writes: "It is literally true that you can succeed best and quickest by helping others to succeed." The best care for weariness is the challenge of helping someone is who even more tired than you.

community

FELLOWSHIP
SOCIAL STRUCTURE ▸ ASSOCIATION ▸ AFFILIATION

UNITY
*SHARED
EXPECTATIONS* ▸ MISSION BASED ▸ ALLEGIANCE

IDENTITY ▸ IDENTIFICATION ▸ DISTINCTIVENESS

chapter

THE ALLIANCE PLAYBOOK DEFINITION OF

community

"FOSTERING A CULTURE OF INTEGRATION AND SHARED EMOTIONAL CONNECTION."

Community is when **Unity** (integration) meets **Fellowship** (emotional connection). Community-minded people share a singular purpose by which they identify with and give their membership in the community a distinctive quality.

community

FELLOWSHIP
SOCIAL STRUCTURE

UNITY
SHARED EXPECTATIONS

IDENTITY
SINGULARITY

Our seventh core value or pillar that holds up the House of The Alliance is Community. In order to demonstrate Community within The Alliance House, one must accept the following formula: **Fellowship + Unity + Identity**. The Alliance measures fellowship by creating a social structure; unity by shared expectations; and identity by encouraging individual input.

albright's answers on community

Merriam Webster definition of Community: an interacting population of various kinds of individuals (such as species) in a common location.

A little girl named Orpah was born on Jan. 29, 1954 in rural Mississippi to a teenage, single mother and was later raised in inner-city Milwaukee. She was named after the biblical figure in the Book of Ruth, but people regularly mispronounced her name because of the unique spelling.

She was molested during her childhood and early teens, became pregnant at 14, had a son who died in infancy and moved to live with a man she calls her father in Tennessee. Despite her tough upbringing, she landed a job in radio during high school and eventually became a local evening news anchor at the age of 19.

Her style quickly grabbed the attention of viewers and producers, which led her to the daytime talk show format at a local station in Chicago, which led to her launching her own production company and into international syndication. You probably know Orpah as Oprah ... as in Oprah Gail Winfrey, a billionaire influencer who created a multi-billion dollar empire and became known as the "Queen of All Media."

Oprah's gift lies in reaching people and making connections that almost anybody can relate to and empathize with, whether it is via her magazine, her TV channel or at speaking engagements.

She has become perhaps the greatest example of how a person can build a community. The Oprah Winfrey Show, which was the highest-rated TV program of its kind from 1986-2011, served as her springboard, which launched her to heights most would have never thought possible. She is frequently at the top of the "Most Influential Women" in the world rankings.

Her ability to talk to viewers and guests led to her building a loyal following that listened to her every word, and often adopted her behaviors like reading the books she read and buying the products she used. Her influence is almost immeasurable.

By the mid-1990s, Oprah pivoted toward literature, self-help and spirituality. Her "community" followed her into those arenas and she picked up even more of an audience and following. Oprah endorsed Barack Obama from 2006-08, and some believe it led to delivering him more than a million votes and helped him win the presidency.

How's that for being influential in your community?

The reach of Winfrey's opinions and her ability to influence people's opinions has been called "the Oprah Effect." It has impacted book sales, beef markets and elections. When she promoted a book, it often shot to No. 1 on best-seller lists.

Oprah became such a trusted voice that she started making guests she liked into their own brands too. Dr. Phil McGraw, Dr. Oz and Rachel Ray all have high-dollar careers based on Oprah endorsing their work.

At her show's peak she drew 13.1 million viewers daily. It aired in 140 countries and she was named America's favorite television personality in 1998, 2000, 2002-06 and 2009 by Harris Poll. Oprah built a community that was wildly popular with women, Democrats, political moderates, Baby Boomers, Gen Xers, etc. Her following was large enough that it allowed her to start the Oprah Winfrey Network.

People love how she uses media and her honesty, which helps her build trust from her community. That trust has allowed her to build a media empire and become a global leader in media and philanthropy. If people like and trust you, then it's likely they will listen and follow you. What are you doing in your circle of influence to gain people's trust? Are you meeting people where they are and then seeking to help them get what they want?

If you are nice to people, can be sincere in your actions and behaviors and take a genuine interest in a person's life, people are going to want to be part of your community. The people with the biggest following are masters at finding ways to connect with people. Over time, if you keep making connections then your circle of influence will be huge. Oprah is a prime example of how to build an audience, a following and a loyal community.

Can you think of some simple and easy ways that you can start making better connections with people going forward? If you can improve on the way you interact with people, then you will be able to grow a larger following and community.

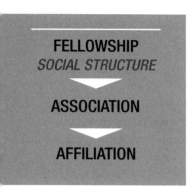

FELLOWSHIP
SOCIAL STRUCTURE

ASSOCIATION

AFFILIATION

Let's now do a deep dive into the formula, starting with Fellowship.

First, community is defined as the area marked by the sentiment of common living. In old French "comunete" means "public spirit." In Latin "communis" means "shared in common." When people in a group feel secure, trusted, and connected -- plus consider themselves partners in creating an environment -- that group can be characterized as having a high level of community.

On the other hand, when people feel threatened, misled, and undervalued in a group, plus act in ways that make others feel the same, the relationships are devoid of companionship or community. This end of the continuum represents society at its worst -- it is what we call "dis-society." Because of the huge energy drain this creates to protect themselves, people do no push to live up to their potential.

Mr. Fred Rogers wrote this about forging a society full of neighborhoods: "Love is at the root of everything, all learning, all relationships. 'Won't you by my neighbor?' is an invitation for somebody to be close to you. The greatest thing we can do is to help somebody know that they are loved, and are capable of loving. I give an expression of care everyday to each child, to help him or her realize that he or she is unique. I end the program by saying, 'You've made this day a special day, by just you being you. There's no person in the whole world like you, and I like you, just the way you are.'"

Mr. Rogers' dream of neighborhoods full of neighbors is best presented by the prerequisite called "Fellowship." The Greeks translated the word "fellowship" to mean essentially a partnership to the mutual benefit of those involved. It is this partnership which serves as the societal cement to the durable relations formed within a solid social structure. This structure which holds the community cement in place, is made up of the friendships formed (Philos Love) and the connections established (relatedness). It is the acting on these friendships which creates fellowship. The act is commonly referred to as "Association."

Association is the act of consorting with or joining with others. There is a strong tendency in human character to the assimilating of itself to that of those with whom it is in contact. There is also a tendency to imitate what we associate with. However, there is a strong probability that, through association with virtuous people, the vicious will, in a degree, be shamed out of their viciousness. This type of positive social arrangement that is formed produces an invitation of inclusiveness which then births the act of collaboration. This collaboration cannot occur without first reconciling a need to "Affiliate."

Affiliation is the first step to making a connection with others. This initial attachment to a group is best represented by the four social bonds it forms. Therefore, the first bond is attachment. It is selective affiliation as a consequence of the development of a social bond. Affiliation is an engagement process due to the social cues being interpreted during the interaction. Social bonding will not occur if these cues are misconstrued. The moral here is: first impressions matter and ignite future bonding. When asked by a reporter why he ran out all fly balls, Joe DiMaggio said: "because there is always some kid who may be seeing me for the first time and I owe him my best."

The second bond is commitment. It refers to our acceptance and willingness to adhere to those societal expectations. Affiliation within a healthy community drives the third bond: Involvement. This type requires participation within the conventional lines of activity. It also requires giving up your time to only "conforming" activities. But this involvement must be driven by the fourth bond: Belief. This is the acceptance of the conventional values and roles of society which control the way we affiliate within a culture.

In summary, in order for us to get future members of The Alliance to believe (trust); we must get them involved (initiative); but before this type of engagement can take place, we must be transparent with our facts in order to gain their commitment (dedication). This loyalty to the task only exists when there is a prior sense of attachment (fondness) to the members within the group. This completes the four-step process of social bonding developed by sociologist Travis Hirschi.

According to Hirschi, in 1969, individuals with strong attachments to others within society are presumed to be less likely to violate societal norms. But conversely, a potential agent with weak attachments is assumed to be unconcerned about the wishes of others, and thereby inclined to deviate from The Alliance expectations (being unlike The Alliance's avatars Aiden or Alice).

Hirschi's commitment construct is based on the premise that there is a correlation between the level of commitment and propensity for dysfunction. Thus, an individual who has invested time, energy, and resources into conforming to Alliance norms and expectations is less likely to deviate than someone who has not made such an investment in their future.

Hirschi then hypothesized that large amounts of involvement spent in socially appropriate activities reduces the time available for distraction. He also contended that involvement such as a job fosters discipline and regiment, which encourages a resolve to resist deviance such as procrastination or wasting of time.

Hirschi's last element of social bonding relates to an individual's level of belief in the moral validity of shared social values and norms found in a functional community. He suggested that persons who strongly believe in the values and norms (like found in The Alliance) are less likely to fall victim to detractors such as family and friends.

FELLOWSHIP

"Without the sense of fellowship with people of like mind…. Life would have seemed to me empty."

- Albert Einstein

Moral: The power of all minds fixed on a common cause is endless and fulfilling.

ASSOCIATION

"He that walks with wise men shall be wise; but a companion of fools shall be destroyed."

- Proverbs 13:20

Moral: Associating with negative people creates negative thought, and associating with positive people creates positive thought.

AFFILIATION

"Unhealthy cultures create addiction. Healthy cultures create social bonds."

- Simon Sinek

Moral: Affiliation based on addiction will eventually turn to confusion and chaos, but affiliation based on a social bond will forever produce clarity and commitment.

albright's answers on fellowship

Few people are familiar with the Biblical figure Nehemiah. He hurried the work of repairing and rebuilding Jerusalem's walls and gates, which he completed in just 52 days in fifth century B.C. following the Babylonian exile. Nehemiah is not just remembered for his record rebuild, but for his efforts in the face of hostile neighbors. Those faithful Jews had to face ridicule and criticism as they began to build the walls. Ridicule can cut deeply, causing discouragement and despair. Instead of trading insults, Nehemiah prayed and kept working. The work prospered because the people had to set their hearts on accomplishing the task. They did not lose heart or give up, but perservered in the work.

Agents will suffer similar ridicule and criticism as they try to build their business. If they keep a mind to work, much good will be accomplished. When ridicule and criticism did not work, the enemies began to threaten warfare against Nehemiah and his workers. We, too, are to wage warfare. Our warfare, however, is not carnal but spiritual. It is built in the spirit of "fellowship." The only thing that can tear down the social structure of fellowship is "compromise." The spirit of compromise is very dangerous to the life of a community. We do not apologize for not compromising our principles. So, that is why it is important at HotSpots (for example) that everyone is cheering and pulling for each other. We can turn our backs, and trust that everyone has our backs. It is important as newcomers come in the room that they feel our sense of community.

There was a time when there were more people against us than for us. But, we redefined our culture to be one of acceptance and inclusion, where love conquers all. This new connection, built on fellowship, created relationships that turned into true friendships. We got tight. We became loyal.

Now, we have a positive peer pressure where encouragement is the norm. We have a social arrangement with each other. It is an invitation to get involved. No judgment and welcomed collaboration is our promise. But, we can't practice a partnership until everyone feels the magic of inclusiveness. We have to include everybody. We have to reach out to the people that are standing in a corner. We also have to avoid, moving forward, the development of cliques. If you collaborate without inclusion, you will birth cliques.

Therefore, it is important early on that we attach new prospects to our community and not the groups that exist within. When I do a HotSpot, I let every new person say their name at the beginning. It changes their world because they're involved in the meeting. My objective is to get them to listen to the next conference call. You're trying to get them to the right business. I'm trying to have him or her commit to going to a meeting. You're trying to get them to sell a policy. Getting someone to go right out of the gate and get a policy issue paid is hard, but getting them to go to a meeting is much easier. You must first get them to the business before they can do the business. They will eventually write a policy. That's why I don't get mad at people being slow to succeed. As long as they're going to the meetings, I know they're eventually going to figure it out.

That's why I say we have a 100 percent success rate. We've never had anybody fail that didn't quit. If they quit associating, if they quit the community, they're going to lose. If they stay in the community, they're going to win. That's why we bust our butts to get people to just hang around so we can love on them. When a person makes that decision to affiliate with us and adhere to our activities, which teaches them not to waste time, they begin to throw away the foolish things that dominate their life of poverty. They come to realize in our culture that "fortune favors the bold," and poverty has great kinship with the timid.

The second part of the formula for community is Unity. It is the state of being one. This oneness builds a feeling of the "collective we" which removes the pressures of how to navigate the terrain of an unfamiliar climate by providing a road map laced with "shared expectations." These expectations both accelerate and transform this concept of unity. When everyone in an organization works toward a common, collective goal, it creates a strong sense of unity.

Everyone must be focused on achieving the same type of objective and have a firm understanding of the contributions of their efforts to the success of the business. As a team, this type of environment is created in our business when directives are clear and goals are defined. When everyone is aware of the shared expectations and is committed to modeling a behavior, then and only then, will unity produce a quality and prosperous outcome.

These shared expectations, which produce unity, will never become a reality until they are "mission-based." The process to create a mission-based community involves distilling a message attached to a "cause." A cause drives awareness, buzz, and action; seemingly sweeping up everyone in its path. Its origin is usually orchestrated, but the emotional appeal is normally organic. Organically, it is something people can get passionate about on a deeply personal level. While there are passionate followers for almost every mission out there, the largest ardent group is made up of the top and the bottom. But both are motivated for very distinctive and different reasons.

The top is motivated to keep what they have, and the bottom is motivated to complain about what they do not have. However, the true power of any organization exists in the middle. These members are the work horses. They do not feel the hard-core connection to the cause of the top or the bottom. The insight here is that these people want to be a part of a community. When your business creates a platform that effectively harnesses the energy of the middle, you will have a significant movement on your hands. It is this type of loyalty of the middle, which sustains an organization's life. Embracing the concept of "allegiance" is the secret code to opening the mystery of unity to any mission-based organization.

This dedication (allegiance) is the act of binding oneself (intellectually and emotionally) to a course of action. This level of commitment comes from a place where members feel an obligation to owe a loyalty debt. This type of support is only realized when the members understand and accept the beliefs/values/norms/roles of the culture. Sharing a common culture is the secret sauce of any community. Just remember: "an allegiance to your future is not possible if your past is your present." Being a faithful servant to a mission-based future is imperative in order to witness a unified society.

How we view our community and how we feel about working where we do builds our allegiance. Be clear that ideas of allegiance – and vows of such – are not new. The human species has always lived and worked in groups. Loyalty – be it to kin groups, nomadic bands, village communities, or tribes – was both expected of people and required for their survival. In order for this tradition to continue and the idea of community to flourish, the concept of "citizen" must supersede a band of individuals.

UNITY

""We all can work, but together we win."

- Ralph Waldo Emerson

Moral: When we forget why we work, we all lose.

MISSION

"Mission is about people, not projects."

- Todd Engstrom

Moral: When we make work all about checking a box and not remembering the people that made that check possible, the mission becomes a shallow victory.

ALLEGIANCE

"Truth is a tyrant – the only tyrant to whom we can give our allegiance. The service of truth is a matter of heroism."

- John F. Kennedy

Moral: Our truth should be demanding of our time and effort when it is tied to a heroic cause.

albright's answers on unity

What makes us a community is our shared expectation that everyone should take care of each other. This desire becomes, "I want you to win as much as I want myself to win." We're not all separate worker bees. We root for each other. The insurance business is usually an individual thing, but The Alliance is a team sport. It's a team sport with our HotSpots; it is when you invite someone to ride along with you to an appointment, it is when you take a phone call on Saturday from someone struggling in the home; and it goes on and on. We need everybody participating in our community by being service-minded. That's what we call "unity."

People move products, products don't move people. The more people you bring to the HotSpots, Instant Thunders, and Conventions, the more products we're going to move. Getting those same people to share a common cause is just one short step away from getting them to share a culture and forming an alliance. You see our very name (The Alliance) represents a bond or connection between individuals in a group. They become allied through an association to further the common interests of the members. This union by relationships turns to an affinity marked by a genuine like of each other. The Alliance is an alliance that fuels our sense of community.

This type of alliance is best reflected by the person that comes and writes $5,000 in the first week, but continues to help set up chairs at a HotSpot meeting. He or she is a team player even though he or she is killing it! That is an example of a healthy person in a healthy community. A person's ego cannot get bigger than their allegiance to the cause. Winning an incentive trip, for example, in a united culture, becomes more than an individual reward, but also an obligation to go and be part of the team.

Alliance vs. Unity: So, what is the difference? Well, alliance is the state of being together or having each other's back, while unity is the state of oneness where the entity cannot become individuals. Simply accepting the idea of "oneness" can have a deep impact on our attitude and mindset. But the implication on us after a strategic "alliance" with something bigger than ourselves, will have a long-lasting effect on our behavior and the depth of our relationships moving forward.

Attitude and mindset are the most important determinants of a person's long-term success. It is more important than skills and much more important than knowledge. If we deeply reflect upon the idea of oneness, it virtually changes how we think and feel about the commitment within The Alliance. In conclusion, this idea of oneness means that being of loving service to another makes perfect and absolute sense when trying to strengthen the alliance of the members.

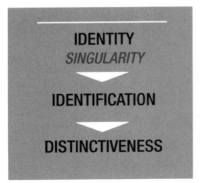

The third part of the formula for Community is Identity. It is the ability to remain the same and be one with yourself as well as the message you stand behind; especially under varying aspects of challenging conditions. This singular purpose embraces our uniqueness and, at the same time, promotes our place in the greater whole. It is part of a person's self-conception and self-perception to find their purpose in life. Accepting one's self allows a person to find fit and placement on a team where one is introduced to a sense of possibility. It is this need for possibility which feeds one's identity.

Carrie Bradshaw said it all when she commented on identity in the very last narrative on the final episode of the "Sex and the City" series: "There are those relationships that open you up to something new and exotic; those that are old and familiar; those that bring up lots of questions; those that bring you somewhere unexpected; those that bring you far from where you started; and those that bring you back. But the most exciting, challenging and significant relationship of all is the one you have with yourself. And if you can find someone to love the you you love, well that's just fabulous." This show taught us how the self-identity and behavior of individuals may be determined or influenced by the terms used to describe or classify them.

"Self-identification" is how you see yourself. But if we are not careful a "stigma" can emerge as a negative label which can change a person's self-concept and social identity. There is, however, a deeper danger that we must be aware of when accepting said labels or bestowing labels upon others. They can start to dictate our behavior and become excuses for self-centered action. Another problem with adopting or using labels is that they can lead to an "us versus them" mindset. It can turn us into victims and result in us seeing our differences as the fault of the other – we can then personalize it, rather than seeing it as a way to understand ourselves and others. But in order to understand ourselves, we need to know what it is we are. This means we must recognize the label as being there, but not internalize the stigma. Labels will remain afterward, if we are not careful. We need to be true to ourselves rather than true to the label.

Most of us see ourselves through our "status." Some perspectives on status emphasize its relatively fixed and fluid aspects. "Ascribed" statuses are fixed for an individual at birth, while "achieved" statuses are determined by social rewards an individual acquires during a lifetime, as a result of the exercise of ability and/or perseverance.

The status that is the most important for an individual, at any given time, is called a "master" status. The master status fundamentally identifies the lens through which an individual shapes their perceptions of self and society. If not careful, a master status can flood out all other aspects of a person's identity. The designation becomes a hindrance to the development of other possible achieved statuses. It becomes the role to which one most relates to the views of oneself, therefore, acting accordingly.

For one to avoid this self-fulfilling prophecy, it is important to grasp the concept of "distinctiveness." It comes from the old French word, "distinctif," meaning markedly individual. In other words, to become distinguishing or distinct is to become an individual. This quality constitutes one's "selfhood." The construction of selfhood is when you first realize your intention and take action as a person with a role to fulfill, along with a purpose to accomplish. This happens when you are able to avoid saying: "Why me?" and start saying: "Why not me?" This is the process of becoming comfortable in your own skin.

"The Eagles'" Don Henley's response to Neil Young in a Rolling Stone magazine article best reiterates this point. Henley said, "It is better to burn out than it is to rust? I don't see rust as a bad thing. I have an old 1962 John Deere tractor that is covered with rust but it runs like a top. The inner workings are just fine. To me, that rust symbolizes all the miles driven, all the good work done, and all the experiences gained. From where I sit, that rust looks pretty damn good."

Recognizing your distinctive value is crucial to identifying your purpose within a singular cause. This is the road map by which a person remains engaged and loyal to a community.

IDENTITY

"That is, the entity, may know itself to be itself and part of the whole; not the whole but one with the whole; and thus retaining its individuality, knowing itself to be itself."

- Edgar Cayce

Moral: You can be a member of a community and still retain your individuality. But you must remember that you are not bigger than the whole.

IDENTIFICATION

"Ego means self-identification with thinking, to be trapped in thought, which means to have a mental image of 'me' based on thought and emotions. So ego is there in the absence of a witnessing presence."

- Eckhart Tolle

Moral: Your past has no power over the present, if you realize deeply that the present moment is all you have. This realization is not possible while ego dominates your objectives. Therefore, your witnessing presence is when you are able to look past what you see in the mirror and rather see what you could be.

DISTINCTIVENESS

"Not your thinking, but your being is distinctiveness."

- C. G. Jung

Moral: Your distinctive qualities are not dependent on what you say you are going to do, but rather simply what you do.

An individual occupies a member of status position, some ascribed (such as sex or race), and some achieved (like educational level or occupation). The master status of an individual is one which, in most or all social situations, will overpower or dominate all other statuses. Know that you are not supposed to stay forever attached to that master status. Yes, you have a certain designation you are proud of, but don't get stuck there Keep moving forward. Gene Simmons of KISS said, "when you've reached the pinnacle of success, start over." Your master status should not be your final designation.

Your tendency to believe that one label or demographic category is more significant than any other aspect of your background, is simply that: a tendency. If you look at master statuses as over-arching achievements one can accomplish in life, one then can define almost any accomplishment as his or her master statuses of choice. In some cases, a person can choose his or her master statuses by consciously projecting certain characteristics, roles, and attributes in their social interactions with others. If you don't like the way people view you within your master status, then change the narrative. For example, when you come to a HotSpot or a bigger event, come correct, come with a spirit of humility. Let people see "the heart of your engine, not the rust on the bottom."

A role is the set of norms, values, behaviors, and personality characteristics attached to a status. Roles and status have a reciprocal relationship; your status affects your role and your role affects your status. If your status is high, say, you're Executive Vice President (EVP), then the roles you fulfill will be equally high and successful. If your status is lowly, say, you're unable to make ends meet, then your roles will be equally low and unsuccessful. The expectancy of a role as to the standard of behavior is so conscious and well-defined that the person playing it has little independence to waver from it (must live up to the expectation). That same person is like an actor on stage delivering dialogue according to the script, waiting for the cue to come from the co-actor (association) and watching the audience's reactions to their it (peer pressure).

For an individual to stop playing a role set by society according to their status, one must see themselves as distinct and unique. The following story provides the proper analogy of how to change the narrative you have been taught, and recognize how to not be a prisoner to it. There were two men who received training on how to survive a bear attack. They were taught to lay down if they encountered a bear in the woods. The two men go in the woods after the training, when they run into an angry bear. One man lays down immediately, but the other takes off running. The man on the ground screams, "why are you running? They didn't tell us to run!" The other man yells back, "I'm trying to survive here. All I have to do is stay ahead of you!" The moral is you have got to stay a step ahead of the competition. Just one step ahead to distinguish yourself is all it takes to stay ahead of someone laying down. Change your role and it changes your status. Change your narrative and it changes your perspective.

THE 4 BEHAVIORS OF

community

KEEP A UNIFIED MINDSET   **BE A GOOD ALLIANCE CITIZEN**

PROMOTE JOINT OWNERSHIP   **PROTECT THE CULTURE**

One of the most important developments an organization can strive for in order to promote growth is establishing a sense of community. We are all social creatures who cannot function effectively without a structure bigger than ourselves. Since about the middle of the 20th century, the term "community" came to describe a manner of uniting, or individuals coming together in order to work toward a noteworthy goal. In present context, community means relationships that are based on trust and respect, a sense of belonging, and individuals working together toward a common vision and understanding how their individual goals align with that vision.

An organization's success has more to do with the clarity of individual roles, recognition of established norms, agreed upon core values, and strength of a belief system rather than with assets, expertise, operating ability, or leadership competence. The Alliance community is looking for people who just want a shot, who are open to change, who understand the value of connecting to a greater whole, and have a deep commitment to ongoing learning and personal growth.

" Alone we can do so little; together we can do so much."

– Helen Keller

Moral: As Buddha once said: "Thousands of candles can be lighted from a single candle." That community candle's life will not be compromised, since its flame is eternal when it burns to a common cause.

Keep A Unified Mindset

KEEP A UNIFIED MINDSET

BE A GOOD ALLIANCE CITIZEN

PROMOTE JOINT OWNERSHIP

PROTECT THE CULTURE

A healthy bottom line is dependent upon the morale within the community of contributors. Morale increases trust, which means that individuals are also less likely to engage in adverse behaviors, which kill the organizational spirit. Building community strengthens morale by creating camaraderie among members of the organization. Camaraderie means that members of the organization feel a sense of friendship and a trust toward one another. One can look at building community as being parallel to "having fun." Plato once said: "You can discover more about a person in an hour of play than in a year of conversation."

The faster we can make new members feel comfortable, and then follow it up with appreciating their efforts; the faster we can grow as an organization. The "fun" aspect allows people to let their guard down and move from living out their meaning to finding their purpose. This discovery of a healthy identity by each individual in The Alliance will create social solidarity within our vision, values, processes and practices. A positive, cohesive organizational culture supported by community building efforts, results in members going above and beyond to get the job done.

Promote Joint Ownership

KEEP A UNIFIED MINDSET   *BE A GOOD ALLIANCE CITIZEN*

PROMOTE JOINT OWNERSHIP   *PROTECT THE CULTURE*

A strong organizational community facilitates learning. A community serves as a means for individuals to share cognitive, emotional, and material resources. Individuals are more comfortable asking questions when the environment is supportive and collaborative as opposed to frigid, stiff, or uncooperative. This promotes the sharing of information such as common attitudes, interests and goals.

People are more likely to give honest feedback when the organization establishes a sense of community. The individual receiving feedback is also more likely to be open-minded and receptive within the same safe environment of a judgement-free community. The bottom line is that individuals with a strong sense of community bonding are likely to work and communicate better.

Being inclusive is a type of participatory decision-making process that requires open communication and the sharing of the thoughts, feelings, and ideas wrapped around the informational data. In communities, more than data is shared – joy, frustration, concern, sympathy, and a contingent of other emotions are just as essential as the data. People must be involved as both thinker and doer. The sense of partnership will create a feeling of fellowship, which in turn, sustains the loyalty to that community.

Be A Good Alliance Citizen

KEEP A UNIFIED MINDSET   *BE A GOOD ALLIANCE CITIZEN*

PROMOTE JOINT OWNERSHIP   *PROTECT THE CULTURE*

First and foremost, don't waste your life sitting in a pew or on the sidelines; or being one of the people that just does enough to get by. This business requires that you be more than a spectator. You must consume what is given from our platform and put it into practice right away. It seems that Sir Isaac Newton got it right with his First Law of Motion: "Bodies at rest tend to stay at rest." Many people just can't seem to get underway and, as a result, they simply don't take action.

Breaking down a goal into small pieces and setting intermediary targets and rewards is sometimes referred to as "chunking." This system involves chipping away at a project. Breaking it down into realistic steps and only doing one at a time allows you to stay in the game and remain focused. Neuroscience tells us that each small success triggers the brain's reward center, releasing feel-good chemical dopamine. This helps with our concentration and inspires us to take another similar step – which in turn advances your drive and new-found ambition.

Let Thomas Edison inspire you on this topic also: "I have not failed. I've just found 10,000 ways that won't work. Our greatest weakness lies in giving up. The most certain way to succeed is always to try just one more time."

Good Alliance citizenship ultimately begins at the grass roots level of "leaning in" and "copying." But this introductory level of involvement does not stop there. Alliance team players, or citizens, are then expected to teach others to lean in and copy. Our Alliance society's success depends upon our middle-level leaders becoming ambassadors of our message, if we are going to properly represent The Alliance. It's not only embracing our values, but each member of The Alliance must also do their part. The work of every member of the whole, however small, is needed. Faithfulness in the little details is a great thing.

M.S. Lowndes writes in his Christian poem, "You have a Part to Play" that, "The only one who matters most is watching for your part, with much anticipation and excitement in His heart. So do not disappoint Him by not taking your cue, though you think is unimportant, this part is made for you."

Protect The Culture

KEEP A UNIFIED MINDSET

PROMOTE JOINT OWNERSHIP

BE A GOOD ALLIANCE CITIZEN

PROTECT THE CULTURE

An organization with a strong sense of community helps foster loyalty. There is a strong correlation between community, loyalty, and The Alliance being successful at retaining agents. Loyal agents that are dedicated to The Alliance will have positive opinions about the organization, which is a powerful form of advertisement. Likewise, one of the best methods of recruitment (if not the best form) is through personal referrals. This means maintaining a great reputation is paramount for any organization.

However, the first step in encouraging others to join our business is to give them something to brag about. A positive, cohesive organizational culture supported by community building efforts results in members going above and beyond to protect the culture. Having agents being proud of our brand is the best medicine for retention. Nothing is a more powerful strategy for attracting and retaining smart and talented individuals than a clear, consistent message; especially if the organization is living that message and promoting the goals for achievement within it.

One of the most damaging ways to kill community spirit and destroy a company's culture is through gossip and rumor. People who indulge in gossip may just be doing it to waste away their time or engage in idle chit-chat with their friends. On the other hand, a person who intends to spread a rumor will seek out specific people and converse with them in order to put the rumor in other people's ears. Whether you unintentionally did not mean to hurt someone with your gossip or purposely spread a rumor with the intent to cause the person harm, both are discouraged and heavily frowned upon at The Alliance.

The excuse that participating in gossip is a good way to increase understanding or knowing beliefs and opinions from the grapevine, will not fly in our culture. The deliberate attempt to spread unverified facts, supported by the excuse that you did not have the time to fact check, will not be tolerated. Gossip and rumors undermine morale, creating negative energy within the organization, and prevents The Alliance from being a unified team.

gratitude

APPRECIATIVE
AFFIRMATION OF GOODNESS ▶ THANKFULNESS ▶ AGREEABLENESS

ALTRUISM
EXHIBITION OF HELPFULNESS ▶ SELFLESSNESS ▶ SPIRITUALITY

ACKNOWLEDGMENT
RECOGNITION OF FORTUNE ▶ INDEBTEDNESS ▶ CONSCIENTIOUSNESS

chapter

THE ALLIANCE PLAYBOOK DEFINITION OF

gratitude

"REMEMBERING WHERE WE COME FROM AND APPRECIATING THE GIFTS BESTOWED UPON US."

Gratitude is when **Acknowledgment** (remembering with recognition) meets **Appreciation** (affirming with thankfulness). Altruistic people who look to exhibit a helpful and selfless nature are typically grateful people as well.

gratitude

APPRECIATIVE
AFFIRMATION OF GOODNESS

ALTRUISM
EXHIBITION OF HELPFULNESS

+

ACKNOWLEDGMENT
RECOGNITION OF FORTUNE

Our eighth core value or pillar that holds up the House of The Alliance is Gratitude. In order to demonstrate gratitude within The Alliance House, one must accept the following formula: **Appreciative + Altruism + Acknowledgment.** The Alliance measures appreciation by affirming goodness; altruism by exhibiting helpfulness; and acknowledgment by recognizing fortune.

albright's answers on gratitude

Merriam Webster definition of Gratitude: the state of being grateful: thankfulness.

I love all of our 8 core values, but my absolute favorite is gratitude. With our previous core values, we selected a historical person to help illustrate the virtues and traits that defined that specific value. For gratitude, I decided to make YOU the person that will personify gratitude from this point on.

Maybe you are thinking that's not possible, but it most certainly is if you decide to show gratitude in all that you do. I'm even going to help you take the first step to make that happen.

Get a sheet of paper out and find a pen ... right now!!! Ask yourself the following two simple questions: What am I grateful for? Why is my heart filled with gratitude?

I want you to spend the next 5-10 minutes writing down your thoughts on gratitude. Keep this paper handy in the coming days so that you can review it daily. Use it as a starting point to help you find ways to express to other people why you are the epitome of what it means to exercise gratitude in your life. There's a quote from Ralph Waldo Emerson that reads, "Cultivate the habit of being grateful for every good thing that comes to you, and to give thanks continuously. And because all things have contributed to your advancement, you should include all things in your gratitude."

I love that quote because it tells you exactly how you should spend your days and time with people. There's so many ways you can show gratitude. When is the last time you wrote a thank you note? Have you called a person you haven't spoken to in a while to tell them how they made a difference in your life or that you appreciate them? Just telling one person thanks for something daily will change your life. I encourage you to find ways to show gratitude to others. Gratitude is an emotion that is closely associated with appreciation in most people's minds. People who operate with a high level of gratitude typically feel like they are part of something bigger than themselves.

When your head and your heart are in the right place, gratitude oozes out of you and people can see it. More importantly, people can feel it too! Gratitude is a powerful emotion that should not be overlooked because of the important role it can play in how successful you are in life and business.

Some of the traits I associate with gratitude are things like praise, recognition, thankfulness, responsiveness, gracefulness, appreciativeness, handshakes, hugs and smiles. When you show another person the right amount of gratitude, it should make them smile and feel warm inside. Gratitude really is a form of love that makes the world a better place. It's a way for you to acknowledge something another person has done for you. Maybe you don't feel worthy of the gift or act bestowed upon you, but you must make every effort to show people you have gratitude in your heart.

Gratitude must be a selfless act. Gratitude must be acts that are done unconditionally to show people you appreciate them, and not because of what they can do for you in return. Gratitude is contagious, however, and the more you show it the more it will be returned to you over time. Even if you don't believe that, it's a powerful law that has been proven time and time again.

Gratitude is an exchange of positive emotion. When somebody performs an act of gratitude, the other person might be motivated to do something gracious for that person or for another person. It's like a chain reaction, or as many would say a way to "pay it forward." Gratitude can be shown to a complete stranger. It doesn't have to be somebody you know. People who show positive gratitude most likely are high-character individuals that are leaders as well. I want you to be the person that people think about when they hear the word gratitude. If you are able to practice gratitude consistently, you will be happier. You will have more self-control and you will be more focused on what is most important to you. I honestly believe you will live an overall better life if you exercise gratitude daily.

If you show other people gratitude, the world will be a better place. Your environment will be healthier and happier. You will have deeper, more meaningful relationships with the people in your life.

I hope you will take time each day to show gratitude because it is a huge component in how The Alliance follows through on the last part of our motto to "Make A Difference." Find ways to show others gratitude and you won't regret it.

Here's the best thing about gratitude: it's free to spread and share with the world! It doesn't cost you a penny. Be grateful in all that you do and celebrate life. Be a cheerleader for a person you know that needs it, or that deserves praise for a job well done. Gratitude can be practiced anywhere and anytime. There's no minimum or maximum when it comes to gratitude.

Practice gratitude!!! You might just be surprised by the benefits that doing so brings to your life.

APPRECIATIVE

AFFIRMATION OF GOODNESS

THANKFULNESS

AGREEABLENESS

Let's now do a deep dive into the formula, starting with Appreciative.

First, the Latin word for gratitude is "gratia" which translates into giving thanks, showing grace, and being grateful. Therefore, gratitude is essentially the recognition of the unearned increments of value in ones experience. The personality traits with the largest correlations with gratitude are: agreeableness, spirituality, and conscientiousness. Having trouble expressing anyone of those traits can affect your ability to express gratitude and be positive with others. Being positive is both a state of being and a perspective. This positivity correlates directly into being grateful. The process occurs when you start remembering what you have (state of being) and valuing it (perspective) at the same time.

Being grateful is an emotion which happens after people receive aide that is thought to be one of these three conditions:

• Costly (Dollars spent): Free leads spotted to new agents (for example)
• Valuable (Aweness Felt): Quality time spent with new agents (for example)
• Kind (Service delivered): Favors to relieve stress of fellow agents (for example)

By releasing your past and regaining your positive outlook, one can reconnect an optimistic perspective to being alive in the consciousness of the above treasures. However, this proper perspective of being appreciative can be blocked by a feeling of hopelessness; not allowing the vital connection to gratitude to materialize into a consciousness of the three treasures. Henry David Thoreau had the best advice to unlock the connection and slay hopelessness when he wrote: "The question is not what you look at, but rather what you see." It is called "relative reflection." It's important to realize things could always be much worse.

According to Cicero: "Gratitude is not only the greatest of virtues, but the parent of all others." Gratitude is also a feeling of happiness that comes from "appreciation" and an expression of thanks. It can be a relationship-strengthening emotion because it requires us to see how we have been supported and affirmed by other people. Gratitude encourages us not only to appreciate gifts, but to repay them (or pay them forward); the sociologist Georg Simmel called it "the moral memory of mankind."

In addition gratitude is an affirmation of goodness. We must recognize the root of this goodness from outside ourselves in order to maintain the goodness inside ourselves. In that vain, gratitude invites a sense of humility and a focus on what truly matters. This focus encourages us to start counting our blessings and be more thankful. "Thankfulness" must be present in order to have an appreciative manner.

Every language in the world has a way of saying "thank you." This is because gratitude is an inherent quality that resides within each human being, and is triggered and expressed spontaneously. This is the counting of the positive things that come our way that we did not actively work toward or ask for. The international Encyclopedia of Ethics defines gratitude as, "the hearts internal indicator on which the tally of gifts outweighs the exchanges." This definition echoes the notion of those unearned increments.

While gratitude is both a feeling and an attitude, thankfulness is the demonstrative expression of it. But this expression of thanks would never take place without an "agreeable" nature. This nature produces a cooperative personality trait which harbors our ability to see the glass half-full. Therefore, agreeableness is considered to be a superordinate characteristic of those individuals that are never expecting, but are highly appreciative. Note: Studies show that agreeable people are more apt to be grateful people. Further, grateful people are happier, less depressed, less stressed and more satisfied with their lives and social relationships.

In conclusion, an agreeable nature allows for an optimistic view of human nature; which in turn leads to not only a thankfulness of what you got, but more importantly, how you got it. This ability to count your blessings creates a true appreciation of the gifts bestowed upon you, and the affirming of the goodness it took to deliver these gifts. This is the true path which produces the virtue of gratitude.

APPRECIATIVE

"Gratefulness is the inner gesture of giving meaning to our life by receiving life as a gift."

- Brother David Steindl-Rast
(a Benedictine monk)

Moral: Seeing life in every breath is the only way to truly appreciate the shot you have been given.

AFFIRMATION

"The roots of all goodness lie in the soil of appreciation for goodness."

- The 14th Dalai Lama

Moral: In order to remain pure of thought, one must affirm the opportunity within the power of goodness with appreciation.

albright's answers on appreciative

Having gratitude and being grateful is about waking up and saying, I got a shot. If I wasn't grateful, I'd just lay in bed and think about my pathetic problems and stuff that happened yesterday. Don't wallow in last week, but rather get up and act like you appreciate the shot God gave you. Gratitude is the value, in my opinion, that holds up the other seven Alliance values. It is the crescendo, a feeling of happiness which is not possible until one learns to appreciate our blessings fully.

When you give back from the appreciation you have experienced, you get this crazy, happy feeling called "serendipity." It is a phenomenon of finding value in something you didn't expect to yield such fortune. This unintentional discovery through chance will soon increase your aptitude for creating desirable results, if you accept the power in being appreciative. It becomes bad luck or bad karma, at this point, if you don't practice appreciation and affirm the goodness bestowed upon you.

In order to be thankful for the gifts conferred, you must also practice "service over self." This motto is based in the Biblical principles found in the Good Samaritan story. The essence of this story is that we are supposed to stop for everyone, and not just who we want to stop for. This is the prerequisite mindset of highly appreciative people.

The precursor of being thankful and showing appreciation afterward, is the concept of agreeableness. If a piece of land appreciates and you want to buy the land, what has to happen first? You must agree with the seller on price. You must come to an agreement before appreciation can take place. When you are hiring somebody, you have to be in an agreement before they can appreciate the opportunity. An agreement allows growth. But, it also allows appreciation to flourish. Finding agreement is the starting point of anything we do. People that are not agreeable have a hard time ever getting started.

Agreeableness and unity is the power of The Alliance. The devil is going to fight us on this. It is going to bring disunity at every single turn. Bringing disagreement to a HotSpot is going to break up any chance of unity; and consequently, the power necessary to combat evil forces will be diminished. A lot of people just want to practice agreeableness without promoting unity. Celebrating what we agree on is easy. Celebrating our differences is tough but is required in order to maintain unity. Because when we celebrate these differences, those same differences never divide us.

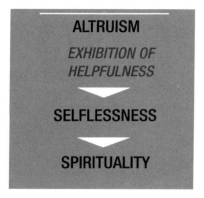

ALTRUISM

*EXHIBITION OF
HELPFULNESS*

SELFLESSNESS

SPIRITUALITY

The second part of the formula for Gratitude is Altruism. Gratitude has been said to mold and shape the whole existence of our entire lives. Martin Luther King, Jr. referred to gratitude as the "basic Christian attitude" and is still referred to today as "the heart of the gospel." It has been suggested by major religious leaders that true, mature and pure intentions come from profound "altruistic" concerns for the welfare of others. Jonathan Edwards claimed that the "affection" of gratitude or finding the "altruism" inside of us is the most precise way to find the evidence of God.

Therefore, a kind heart or spirituality (concern for the human spirit) is the prerequisite when trying to become selfless (searching for an opportunity to honor) – which allows us to endorse generosity with altruism (exhibiting a helpful nature).

Gratitude is like a skill, which can be trained to take place. With practice and the right perspective, there will always be many things to be grateful for. Perhaps the key reason we do not make gratitude a part of our daily lives is the distractions of modern life have simply made it all too easy to forget gratitude's importance; and also our basic lack of "selflessness" (honoring the opportunity).

By diligently engaging with systematic reminders, we can discover a conscious practice of recognizing and remembering where we came from and who was responsible for getting us here. With this selfless attitude, gratitude transforms into a disposition, which is then one step away from a habit or tendency. This daily practice of gratitude keeps the heart open regardless of what comes our way which distracts us.

We need not settle for our present disconnection from the healthy, life-affirming and uplifting human experience of gratitude. When people in great numbers choose to practice it, the cumulative force generated can create the kind of world we all hope for and desire. This concern for human spirit aims to recover the original shape of sacred meaning as it embodies the concept of contentment (harmony and peace of mind). Some people spend their whole life building their body or building a collection, but they should be trying to build their "spirituality." It is the only thing that remains eternal.

Spiritual development, or awakening, and reduction of our ego is the main gain to applying gratitude to our lives. The practices of moral virtue and altruistic behvavior are important paths toward spiritual awareness and growth. As we pursue these ways of being, we gradually become less self-centered and more connected in a harmonious way with ourselves, others, and the world.

Why is ethical behavior considered to be so important in relation to our spiritual development? I would like to suggest the following reasons:

Firstly, behaving ethically promises an inner state of well-being and serenity. In practicing moral virtue we will become more content and at peace within ourselves and in our lives. Inner peace is a foundation for spiritual growth, and in turn, makes it easier to practice gratitude.

Secondly, service to others is another common principle and practice in relation to spirituality. Altruism and compassion are characteristics of being spiritually awakened. Service is a principle common to all major spiritual traditions. Therefore, altruism, when put into practice, promotes love without attachment to our ego. Spiritually speaking, the practice of love and gratitude is quite often viewed as a way of connecting us to our true nature. The connecting nature of altruism is expressed by author Steve Taylor in the following quote: "Practicing self-sacrifice and altruism opens us up to God, because the nature of God is love. Our own nature becomes attune to God's and we become one with it."

ALTRUISM

"Every man must decide whether he will walk in the light of creative altruism or in the darkness of destructive selfishness."

- Martin Luther King, Jr.

Moral: Everyday is judgment day (light has come into the world). This is the judgment: Life's most persistent and urgent question is, "What are you doing for others?" Further, when there is a conflict, creative altruism is more than an outcome, it is a process that results in win/win results for everyone. And it is a process that creates and requires constant dialog.

HELPFULNESS

"No one is useless in this world who lightens the burdens of another."

- Charles Dickens

Moral: You are suddenly relevant when you decide to help another get what they need and want out of life.

albright's answers on altruism

Altruism is evidence of God's love and compassion. It is also about not being worried about yourself and practicing "inconvenience." Leadership is about embracing the burden of going to a HotSpot far away from your home in order to impact new faces with your presence. It is about getting outside your comfort zone and being inconvenienced. The daily practice of gratitude keeps our heart open, no matter what hardships come our way; and altruism, if internalized, will aide in not allowing your heart to shut down.

Mr. Rogers had a technique that helped jump start your heart of gratitude: "The greatest gift you can give others is the gift of your honest self. Who in your life had been such a servant to you? Who has helped you have the good that grows within you? Let's close our eyes and think of those who love and loved us and want and wanted the best for us in life. Let's think about the ones that have helped us get to this point in life. You didn't get here by accident. Can you see these people that have made a difference in your life? No matter where they are, whether nearby, far away, or in heaven; just imagine how pleased those people are or would be that you have thought of them right now. We all have the choice of encouraging others. Now, lastly, think about all the people you have helped in life's journey. I hope the list is long but most important I hope it grows longer after this."

The most miserable people you know are people of entitlement. These people have a "You owe me" mentality. They are all surface people with no balance in their life. They will never know contentment until they receive the gift of spirituality. People think they must first change their habits, and their behaviors. But, spirituality (balance) starts with changing your thinking.

You will never have peace, joy, harmony, or feel whole; until you find something bigger than yourself. Then, and only then, will the light inside you be turned on. That's when you will be flooded with true happiness.

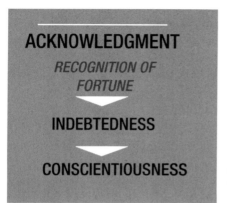

ACKNOWLEDGMENT

RECOGNITION OF FORTUNE

INDEBTEDNESS

CONSCIENTIOUSNESS

The third part of the formula for Gratitude is Acknowledgment. Gratitude is a feeling that emerges within. However, it is not simply an emotional response; it is a choice we make. We can choose to recognize the fortune bestowed upon us, or we can choose to be ungrateful by taking our gifts and blessings for granted. Please don't make this mistake.

For philosopher David Hume, ingratitude is "the most horrible and unnatural crime that a person is capable of committing." For philosopher Immanuel Kant, it is, quite simply, "the essence of vileness." Ingratitude, which of course, has become the norm, corrodes social bonds and undermines public trust, leading to societies built on rights and entitlements rather than duties and obligations, and societies built on "me" rather than "us."

Despite the great and many benefits that gratitude confers through simple "acknowledgments," gratitude is hard to cultivate because it opposes itself to deeply ingrained human traits. In particular, our striving to better our lot; our need to feel in control of our destiny; and our propensity to credit ourselves for our success can kill potential gratitude when wrongly paired with blaming others for our failures, and our belief in some sort of cosmic equality or justice (thinking somebody owes you something). You must possess an indebted feeling or a sense of responsibility in order to be loyal to the acknowledgment you are validating or paying homage to.

Gratitude is a value-receiving, inward-focused energy. It takes something that is happening externally to bring it inward. It does not really require any outward action other than this initial external happening, which spurs the inward motivation on. Afterward, you can fully express extreme gratitude as well as receive its intrinsic benefits.

On the other hand, "indebtedness" is a feeling creating outward focused energy. In order to experience the inward gift of gratitude, one must first accept, with emotional maturity, the required outward response of saying or parroting "thank you" and not actually really meaning it. Therefore, indebtedness is just plain good manners, and returning a favor becomes the decent thing to do. But an obligation to humankind or this thing called "conscientiousness" is required to execute a returning of a favor (indebtedness).

In general, "conscientiousness" implies a desire to do a task well (being careful and vigilant while doing it). But when paired with the expectation of indebtedness, conscientiousness takes on the dimension of being both dutiful and obligated while returning that favor. Being disorderly and showing a lack of self-discipline has a direct negative impact on your ability and desire to exhibit a grateful nature. In order to recognize the importance of the kind act done for you, one must already possess a deliberate thoroughness in their own lives.

In other words, one must be diligent in looking for kind acts in order to recognize their impact. Once appreciated from outward sources, a person can ignite the inward goodness that rests inside each one of us. This inward acknowlegement draws its motivation to act from a feeling of indebtedness, which causes a grateful spirit to come out.

ACKNOWLEDGMENT

"I believe that if you don't derive a deep sense of purpose from what you do, if you don't come radiantly alive several times a day, if you don't feel deeply grateful at the tremendous good fortune that has been bestowed on you, then you are wasting your life. And life is too short to waste."

- Srikumar Rao

Moral: It is not the feeling of indebtedness which makes it a virtue, it is the expression of indebtedness through your action, through your repayment, which makes it virtuous.

RECOGNITION

"The invariable mark of wisdom is to see the miraculous in the common."

- Ralph Waldo Emerson

Moral: The true fortunate ones are those who can marvel in the last breath they just took.

albright's answers on acknowledgment

Your job is to move and not attack. Crediting our own movement kills our ability to have gratitude. Remembering what others have done for you and trying not to remember what you done for them, is the first step to guarding your ability to show gratitude. It is your choice to deliver this acknowledgment or to merely keep it floating around your mind, ignoring the urge to say a simple "thank you."

It takes courage to deliver a heartfelt and authentic acknowledgment, because it makes you feel vulnerable. But in fact, it should make you have a sense of indebtedness, motivating you to repay favors received and level inequities imparted. We know that no debt or owing can carry an experience of joy, but rather a sense of freedom from the obligation being delivered. Do not get confused with gratitude and indebtedness. Gratitude is an expression of love, and indebtedness is rooted in guilt.

Guilt cannot equate to love, for love has no guilt. While love requires no guilt to repay a debt, it is guilt that feeds the conviction to repay the debt, and in turn, gives us the confidence to practice love. When people say, "I am indebted to you forever," it might start out as stress connected to obligation; but once the act of repayment is experienced, the pride internalized quickly turns into a feeling of dutiful love.

What you are loyal to soon becomes what you are indebted to. For example, people don't appreciate their HotSpot until they learn to properly acknowledge their mentor. When you fight our leaders and the system, it is evidence of no indebtedness. This conscientiousness does not occur by accident. It is realized with a deliberate nature on your part. For example, you should go into a client's home with the intention to help the client, to get a check, get referrals, get a green sheet, and to recruit. Being conscious of this obligation is the best way to demonstrate your gratitude for the opportunity that The Alliance has provided you.

This consciousness of gratitude is not so much a way of thinking as it is a way of being. It is not something we achieve as much as allow. One thing's for sure: when you get a taste, you want more. When we practice acceptance of what is, when we appreciate the power of right now, gratitude seems to seep up through the cracks between our thoughts like ground water. When everything becomes what it is supposed to be, in that special moment, you can then experience the calmness that is the reward of the consciousness of gratitude.

THE 4 BEHAVIORS OF

gratitude

SHOW APPRECIATION

COUNT YOUR BLESSINGS

PRACTICE INDEBTEDNESS

HONOR THE OPPORTUNITIES

While the importance of gratitude was not recognized until recently, ancient and not-so-ancient philosophers such as Cicero, Seneca, and Adam Smith preached its importance. Cicero and Seneca thought of gratitude as a crucially important virtue, which was fundamental to a successful civilization.

Gratitude is a human emotion that can be most simply defined as appreciation or acknowledgment of an altruistic act. It is a way for people to appreciate what they have instead of always reaching for something new, in the hopes it will make them happier or thinking they can't be satisfied until every physical and material need is met. Gratitude helps people refocus by acknowledging what they have instead of what they lack. And, although it may feel contrived at first, this mental state grows stronger with use and practice.

Learning to stop feeling sorry for yourself is difficult. But while it can be hard to avoid self-pity entirely, mentally strong people choose to exchange self-pity for gratitude. Whether you choose to write a few sentences in a gratitude journal, or simply take a moment out of your day to silently acknowledge that things could be much worse; giving thanks can transform your life. As writer Alexis de Tocqueville once described it, gratitude is "a habit of the heart."

Expressing gratitude is transformative, just as transformative as expressing complaint. In order to reject complaint and accept gratitude requires a changing of perspective. It's the little me against the rest of the world. The little me sees itself as being entitled to something. The world owes me something.

But, really what on earth does the world owe you when it comes down to it? Absolutely nothing!

"Gratitude is riches. Compliant is poverty."

– Doris Day

Moral: Once you stop complaining and start being grateful, the light that shines on your life will soften your heart and open your mind; revealing truths that have been hidden from view and leading you toward a richer, more joyful and fulfilling life.

Show Appreciation

SHOW APPRECIATION

COUNT YOUR BLESSINGS

PRACTICE INDEBTEDNESS

HONOR THE OPPORTUNITIES

Gratitude is an emotion expressing appreciation for what one has – as opposed to an emphasis on what one wants or thinks they need. Half-hearted "thank you" will not do; deep gratitude has to come from within in a meaningful way. William James, well known psychologist and philosopher said, "the deepest principle of human nature is to be appreciated." If we are honest with ourselves, we all want to feel valued for who we are and recognized for our contributions and accomplishments. It's important for us to know that we have made a difference in someone's life.

You should challenge yourself daily to make your expression of appreciation stand out from the crowd. Make sure it is genuine and something that will make an impression. While going the extra mile is admirable, don't forget the simple little things we can do on a daily basis to let people know they are appreciated. Author Robert Cavett writes, "Three billion people on the face of the earth go to bed hungry every night, but four billion people go to bed every night hungry for a simple word of encouragement and recognition."

When you express your approval or gratitude for something they have done, you will not only enhance their lives, you will enrich yours as well. One of the laws of the universe states that what you give, you get in return. It costs little or nothing, and it almost follows suit that people will demonstrate their gratitude for what you do. When you show an interest in others by noticing the good things they've done, they will attract to you like a magnet.

Showing appreciation will also accelerate the building process of any relationship. It will then increase your value to the market. When you show your appreciation to others, their respect for you will grow and so will your influence as a leader. It's a free form of currency. People will do more for recognition than they will for money. Show them you care and they will be loyal to you, even if better opportunities come their way.

Practice Indebtedness

SHOW APPRECIATION   *COUNT YOUR BLESSINGS*

PRACTICE INDEBTEDNESS   *HONOR THE OPPORTUNITIES*

Feeling grateful starts with an acknowledgement that life is good and rewarding. This can be motivating. Waking up in the morning and repeating, "It's great to be alive," is a good place to start. This emotion that life is abundant, makes a person feel grateful toward others. There is also utility in gratitude such as making amends or solving issues at hand. Reciprocity is not needed in feeling gratitude. The receiver is compelled to pay the goodness forward, generating positivity all around.

This positivity or conscientiousness of being in the moment, conversely produces a feeling of indebtedness. Gratitude soon follows this chain of events when, especially, the benefactor has no agenda, has low expectations of return from the beneficiary, and is selfless, sincere, and voluntary. It has been found in studies that increasing expectations communicated by a benefactor will not cause the beneficiaries to be likely to help the benefactor in the future. It is for this reason and it has been argued, that the debt of gratitude is internally generated, and is not due to an economic form of indebtedness.

However, if gratitude is an emotion that originates from an internal motivation, then indebtedness is an emotion that originates from external motivation. Both gratitude and indebtedness are associated with the intention to repay for the received benefit. The need to reciprocate is driven, first, by outside forces, such as the perceived value and effort put forth in the act; which, in turn, then stirs the external urgency to even the score. The internal feeling of gratitude follows with a motivation driven by guilt to practice indebtedness.

Count Your Blessings

SHOW APPRECIATION   **COUNT YOUR BLESSINGS**

PRACTICE INDEBTEDNESS   *HONOR THE OPPORTUNITIES*

Counting your blessings is a reminder to be grateful. It is a call to rise above the discouragement in order to reach a new appreciation for the blessings bestowed upon you. Where there is absence of gratitude, there is a presence of vanity. However, grateful people have an easier time accepting the basic premises of life, which creates a healthy perspective:

Life is not fair: accepting this premise means you will never be disappointed.

No one owes you anything: accepting this premise means you don't see the golden rule as an insurance policy.

No one was put here to make you happy: accepting this premise means you have graduated to self-worth.

Blessings are not meant to be measured or counted. Numbers are for things and blessings are not things. Blessings are sacred gifts. Therefore, counting your blessings does not mean tally them up. Rather, counting your blessings means be aware of their presence. Appreciate their presence. Just for a moment, count your blessings instead of adding up your troubles. There's always something to be thankful for, no matter our circumstances. Sometimes, we just need to shift our perceptions. To live at all is miracle enough. Elizabeth Gilbert writes, "you have to participate relentlessly in the manifestations of your own blessings." We don't have to wait for a tragedy to happen before we become willing to shift our perceptions and see with new eyes the beauty we missed before.

In Dr. Wayne Dyer's wise words: "Miracles come in moments. Be ready and willing." It's not our task to create miracles, but be thankful for the opportunity to live within one. Therefore, counting your blessings is really another way of saying, "enjoy your life fully." Suffering gives us another chance to shift our perspective. The shift, then, becomes the real miracle. You don't need to feel gratitude toward what you have now, but rather for what you have when you have nothing.

Honor The Opportunities

SHOW APPRECIATION   COUNT YOUR BLESSINGS

PRACTICE INDEBTEDNESS   **HONOR THE OPPORTUNITIES**

It's not just that we feel grateful, or that we express our gratitude, but that we actually experience a sincere desire to honor the opportunity put in front of us. It is a sense of honor that arises naturally within us as we recognize how we have been fortunate and supported by others. This recognition needs to be repaid with our deeds and demonstrated through a tremendous work ethic. This was never made more clear than in Colossians 3:23-24. It reads, "Whatever you do, work heartily as for the Lord and not for men, knowing that from the Lord you will receive the inheritance as your reward. You are serving the Lord Christ."

One of the greatest ways to honor the opportunity is by keeping our promises and covenants. A man or woman unable to do this is fundamentally worthless. If your word is not supported by action or if you take a cavalier attitude toward your obligations of gratitude, then the party's over. You may as well stick a fork in your reputation, because no one will respect your ungrateful spirit. It's like having a stain on your reputation and character that no amount of bleach could ever remove. The saddest part of it all is that this damage manifested from a selfish nature.

Voltaire writes about gratitude as a way of honoring: "Appreciation is an excellent thing. It makes what is excellent in others belong to us as well." Accepting reality leads toward the first step of being grateful. Being unable to appreciate the playing field will keep you blind to the opportunity. Learning to love the weather you get is not resignation, but being smart. It doesn't mean stop loving a sunny day; simply to embrace the rain too.

This recognition of the truth in the moment allows you to play through the bad weather or times in life, in order to honor the sunshine; when it appears, in concert with your gratitude.

value perception profile

PART 1: INSTRUCTIONS

Allocate **3** points between the two alternative reasons in each pair. Base your point allocation on your judgment of relative importance; indicating your preference of value bases. Allocate the points between the first item and the second item based on perceived importance in the following fashion:

A	C	E	G
_3_	_2_	_1_	_0_
B	D	F	H
_0_	_1_	_2_	_3_

Be sure that the numbers assigned to each pair add up to 3
None of the combinations can be 1.5 and 1.5.

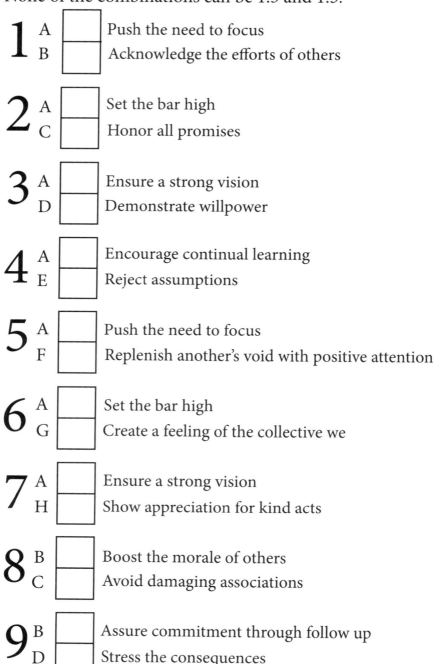

1   A [   ]   Push the need to focus
    B [   ]   Acknowledge the efforts of others

2   A [   ]   Set the bar high
    C [   ]   Honor all promises

3   A [   ]   Ensure a strong vision
    D [   ]   Demonstrate willpower

4   A [   ]   Encourage continual learning
    E [   ]   Reject assumptions

5   A [   ]   Push the need to focus
    F [   ]   Replenish another's void with positive attention

6   A [   ]   Set the bar high
    G [   ]   Create a feeling of the collective we

7   A [   ]   Ensure a strong vision
    H [   ]   Show appreciation for kind acts

8   B [   ]   Boost the morale of others
    C [   ]   Avoid damaging associations

9   B [   ]   Assure commitment through follow up
    D [   ]   Stress the consequences

10 B □ Embrace cause over self
   E □ Show humility

11 B □ Acknowledge the efforts of others
   F □ Notice another's distress

12 B □ Boost the morale of others
   G □ Cultivate a feeling of fellowship

13 B □ Assure commitment through follow up
   H □ Promote life as a gift

14 C □ Honor all promises
   D □ Own all actions

15 C □ Avoid damaging associations
   E □ Practice empathy over evaluation

16 C □ Show no favoritism
   F □ Connect emotionally to the sufferer

17 C □ Establish authenticity
   G □ Increase level of involvement through leaning in

18 C □ Establish authenticity
   H □ Affirm the gifts bestowed

19
D ☐ Demonstrate willpower
E ☐ Emphasize manners

20
D ☐ Stress the consequences
F ☐ Alleviate another's pain

21
D ☐ Own all actions
G ☐ Display loyalty

22
D ☐ Exhibit initiative
H ☐ Honor opportunities by working diligently

23
E ☐ Practice empathy over evaluation
F ☐ Notice another's distress

24
E ☐ Emphasize manners
G ☐ Create a feeling of the collective we

25
F ☐ Connect emotionally to the sufferer
G ☐ Cultivate a feeling a fellowship

26
H ☐ Show appreciation for kind acts
E ☐ Reject assumptions

27
H ☐ Promote life as a gift
F ☐ Alleviate another's pain

28
H ☐ Affirm the gifts bestowed
G ☐ Increase level of involvement through leaning

PART 2: RESULTS

In order to score your questionnaire, go back through the instrument and add up all the scores that you have given to each of the A, B, C, D, E, F, G, and H items. Enter the total for each category in the boxes below. As a check on your addition, the total of these scores should equal 84.

totals:

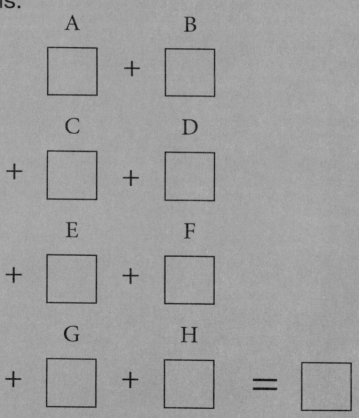

PART 3: SCORING SHEET

Transfer your score totals from the results and plot them on the graph below by circling the corresponding number on each scale. Connect the circled points to complete your profile. This provides feedback on your perception of the relative strength of each of your value bases.

A	B	C	D	E	F	G	H
21	21	21	21	21	21	21	21
20	20	20	20	20	20	20	20
19	19	19	19	19	19	19	19
18	18	18	18	18	18	18	18
17	17	17	17	17	17	17	17
16	16	16	16	16	16	16	16
15	15	15	15	15	15	15	15
14	14	14	14	14	14	14	14
13	13	13	13	13	13	13	13
12	12	12	12	12	12	12	12
11	**11**	**11**	**11**	**11**	**11**	**11**	**11**
10	**10**	**10**	**10**	**10**	**10**	**10**	**10**
9	**9**	**9**	**9**	**9**	**9**	**9**	**9**
8	8	8	8	8	8	8	8
7	7	7	7	7	7	7	7
6	6	6	6	6	6	6	6
5	5	5	5	5	5	5	5
4	4	4	4	4	4	4	4
3	3	3	3	3	3	3	3
2	2	2	2	2	2	2	2
1	1	1	1	1	1	1	1

A=	B=	C=	D=	E=	F=	G=	H=

conclusion

Core values toward the common good can help restore a sense of unity, not only in The Alliance but the U.S. as well. Everyone should know clearly what our core values are and why we have them. The core values learned about in this book, show who we really are. It is our hope that these values guide your choices moving forward.

Gandhi once said, "Your beliefs become your thoughts, your thoughts become your words, your words become your actions, your actions become your habits, your habits become your values, your values become your destiny."

In our personal life, the decisions we make define our destiny. The same concept applies to business. A company is guided by its core values. It's not hard to make decisions when you know what your values are. At The Alliance, our 8 core values as well as the accompanying 32 behavioral expectations are the foundation of what we as a company aspire to become.

We truly believe our values and behaviors can set The Alliance apart from the competition by clarifying its identity and serving as a structural guideline for our staff and agents. Now that you have completed this book, it is our wish that you will become an ambassador for this great organization. Remembering what you do and how you do it matters. Members of The Alliance, rookies and veterans alike, are watching you uphold these values and behaviors. It is all of our responsibility to ensure that everyone entering our door of P.I.E. are welcomed and afforded the same opportunities that we have experienced thus far.

The Alliance culture is the epitome of positivity and advancement. It is our people that support a culture by living a code of conduct defined by our values and behaviors found in this book. If you want to leave a Godly legacy, you must first determine what you believe in -- what is most important to you. And then you need to evaluate how well you are living according to our value system, because you are being watched. Your actions and lifestyle mean more than your words.

about the authors

ANDY S. ALBRIGHT

Andy Albright is an entrepreneur, business owner, author, motivational speaker and the host of Season 2 of Amazon Prime's Self Made show.

Albright co-founded National Agents Alliance (aka The Alliance) in 2002 and quickly helped it grow into one of the country's largest and most successful insurance marketing organizations, specializing in life event marketing and sales insurance marketing organization in the United States. As the top seller with companies like Mutual of Omaha, Transamerica and Foresters, The Alliance posts $100 million in sales annually.

Andy has appeared in regional North Carolina magazines and newspapers, and his company was selected from a pool of 35,000 area businesses as the N.C. Triad's Fastest Growing Company by Greensboro's Triad Business Journal in 2007. Albright was named to the Triad's 2011 Movers & Shakers list by Business Leader magazine, and has appeared on several national radio shows. Most recently, Albright was named 2018 "Man Of The Year" by the Boys Scouts of America for his contribution to scouting.

Albright is the author of "The 8 Steps to Success," "Millionaire Maker Manual" and "Inside The Circle."

Albright is the namesake of the Albright Entrepreneurs Village (AEV), a place for NC State students who want to learn to think like an entrepreneur. The AEV is a residential community on campus that involves residents from all majors and provides social and co-curricular activities to engage them in the startup world and encourage them to develop their ideas and ventures. This diverse group receives coaching from successful entrepreneurs and immersion in the programs that help students translate ideas into action.

Albright is a member of the advisory board for NC State's

Entrepreneurship Initiative, a member of the advisory board for the NC State University Engagement and a loyal supporter and major donor of Wolfpack athletics. Albright is a motivational speaker for various groups and organizations. He is passionate about helping mentor entrepreneurial-minded students and aspiring job creators.

Andy and his wife, Jane live in Union Ridge, N.C. They have two children – Haleigh and Spencer.

about the authors

JEFF BRIGHT

Jeff Bright is the Cultural Advisor to The Alliance. He worked part-time for six years prior to joining the team full-time. During his tenure at The Alliance, Bright has served as a speaker and teacher at all events and conventions. He also helps coach the staff and agents alike. He is especially noted for designing and administering personality inventory profiles, which provide valuable insight to all members of The Alliance family, by measuring their strengths and weaknesses.

Bright worked previously at Alamance Community College (ACC) for 30 years as Vice President for Corporate Education, where he retired in 2017. In his role as Vice President, Bright consulted and coached more than 300 companies and organizations. While at ACC, he also taught sociology in the college transfer program.

Bright received his undergraduate from Wingate College with a B.S. in history. He also received his Master's degree in education and sociology at the University of North Carolina at Greensboro. Bright co-authored three books on the American Revolutionary War, and is responsible for erecting two historical markers.

He is married to Nancye and has two step-children, Adam and Lauren. Jeff and his wife are contributors to the Conservators Center in Burlington, N.C., where they have adopted two animals. At home, they are the parents to eight rescue cats.

resources

Millionaire Maker Manual
by Andy Albright
Retail $29.95

Go to *shoptheAlliance.com* to get yours today!

ANDY ALBRIGHT CD SERIES

5 Ways To Stay Positive

life, we all face challenges. Andy will give 5 strategies to stay positive when you face obstacles.

How To Overcome It All

Life is filled with struggles and you have to overcome the obstacles of life or your will get stuck in the mess.

MOVE - Volume 1

his mix tape-style audio will help you start ur day off right or get your mind right when you are riding in your car or working out.

MOVE - Volume 2

The follow up to MOVE 1, this mix tape features short inspirational tracks to inspire you no matter what you are doing.

Thrive

Go to ShoptheAlliance.com to get yours today!

his 3-disc set of audios offers high-level training to help you grow and avoid procrastination.

ALLIANCE PODCASTS

GET NEW EPISODES
AUTOMATICALLY TO YOUR DEVICES

GOOGLE PLAY   PODCAST   STITCHER

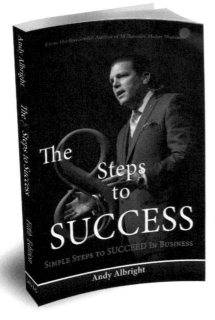

The 8 Steps To Success
by Andy Albright

Simple Steps To SUCCEED In Business

Go to ShopTheAlliance.com to get yours today!

WOULDN'T YOU LIKE TO ACQUIRE THE MINDSET AND HABITS THAT MAKE ANDY ALBRIGHT SO SUCCESSFUL? THE MORE YOU KNOW, THE MORE YOU'LL GROW INTO THE PERSON YOU WERE MEANT TO BECOME.

VISIT ANDYALBRIGHT.COM

and subscribe to receive alerts on Andy's latest thoughts, ideas and blog articles, sent automatically to your email inbox!

SUBSCRIBE AT ANDYALBRIGHT.COM!

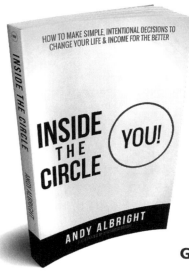

INSIDE THE CIRCLE
by Andy Albright

HOW TO MAKE SIMPLE. INTENTIONAL DECISIONS TO BETTER YOUR LIFE AND INCOME.

Go to ShopTheAlliance.com to get yours today!

KEEP UP WITH ANDY!

LIKE ON FACEBOOK

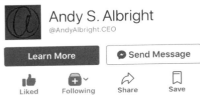

Andy S. Albright
@AndyAlbright.CEO

Learn More   💬 Send Message

👍 Liked   ➕ˇ Following   ↪ Share   🔖 Save

Author • Burlington, North Carolina

FOLLOW ON TWITTER

PRESIDENT AND CEO OF
The Alliance

Following

Andy S. Albright
@AndySAlbright

I encourage people to DO today what others won't so
they can live tomorrow like others can't !

📍 Burlington, NC   🔗 andyalbright.com
📅 Joined April 2009

1,398 Following   **3,098** Followers

Tweets   Tweets & replies   Media   Likes

FOLLOW ON INSTAGRAM

andysalbright

597 posts   **1,838** followers   **78** following

Message   👤✓

Andy Albright
A guy who Just wanted A SHOT!!!
Encouraging others to DO what others
won't DO SO they can live tomorrow like
others can't!
www.amazon.com/gp/video/detail/
B07JLCL8GN

IGTV   N247RU   Thoughts   NC State

SUBSCRIBE ON YOUTUBE:

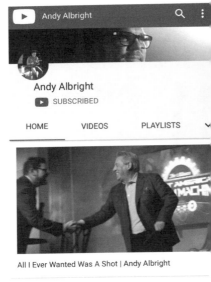

Andy Albright

Andy Albright
▶ SUBSCRIBED

HOME   VIDEOS   PLAYLISTS

All I Ever Wanted Was A Shot | Andy Albright

@AndySAlbright